COMPANY AND POSITION SPECIFIC INTERVIEW PREP

How You Too Can Get Job Offers from Microsoft, Amazon, Google, Uber, Facebook And Many More

COMPANY AND POSITION SPECIFIC INTERVIEW PREP

How You Too Can Get Job Offers from Microsoft, Amazon, Google, Uber, Facebook And Many More

Kunal Chopra

Founder and CEO of Coursetake

www.coursetake.com

Author, Executive, Educator, Investor, Entrepreneur

CEO, COO, GM, VP, Director, Senior Manager, Fortune 100 Hiring Manager, MBA, MS, BE

Amazon, Microsoft, Groupon, Unikrn, NISA, Bridgewater Associates, Techstars, All Star Directories

First Printing: 2017

ISBN 978-1978493797

KCSM LLC
10704 Eastridge Drive NE,
Redmond, WA, 98053

www.coursetake.com

Dedication

To my family – Sonal, Buddy, Sam, Mum, Dad, Mom, Aryan, Krish, Coco, and Kiaan. You give me the inspiration everyday to be my best.

Thank you. Without your support and patience I would have never achieved my dream.

This book is 35 years of your hard work.

Table of Contents

Bookmark not defined.

Acknowledgements

I would love to take a moment to thank Sonal. Thank you very much for everything and being there to push me.

I would also like to thank my online mentors – Brendan Buchard and Tony Robbins. I have applied the concepts of personal development and peak performance that you taught me to my own career and now have been blessed to share these with the whole wide world.

Finally, one man who changed my life ever since I met him – Shaun Thomas. Love you and adore you from the bottom of my heart. Thanks for pushing me.

Preface

Hi friends,

My name is Kunal Chopra and I'd like to welcome you to this book. This book is not just a narrative of my own life, but it is a comprehensive guide to ensure that you will absolutely ace your upcoming interview. And I don't just mean getting a job offer. Anyone can do that. I mean truly walking into that interview room and blowing away your interviewers to the extent that they do not have an option but to give you an excellent job offer. I mean putting you in a position of such leverage that you can pretty much command any salary that you like. By the end of this book, I'd like you to walk out with tons of tools to become an absolute winner when it comes to interviewing.

This book doesn't only focus on interview questions and answers. It does a lot more than that. Answering questions is only a small piece of the puzzle to ace an interview. We will cover that, not to worry, but to truly ace your interview, you will need to work on several other things. You must work on yourself and on your confidence, you will need to master the art of selling, you will need to learn to conduct market research on the industry, the company, and a lot more.

However, before we get started I'd like to tell you a little bit about myself and my story.

I came to the United States 15 years ago to pursue a Masters in Computer Science from Clemson University. I had recently completed my Bachelors in Computer Engineering from The University of Mumbai and was using this move to take my education to the next level.

During that time, I graduated with a 4.0/4.0. I was the only student in a class of 100 to get that score. In short, I was an absolute A student. I don't say this to you to impress upon you my credentials, but to show to you that there was no reason an employer wouldn't hire me with those credentials and profile after graduation. Boy, was I wrong!

When it came to the interview process and getting jobs, I was a complete failure. I would continue to apply to tons of opportunities, mostly online, one after the other, but none would come my way. The few that did give me a chance to speak with them over the phone, I failed so badly at that I wondered how I even graduated with those numbers. On the other hand, everyone else in my class got opportunities with some of the best companies in the world. But I was sitting there jobless with the only claim to fame being my degree with straight A's.

Six months went by of consistent failure and rejection before I started closely reflecting on what went wrong and why, despite having stellar academic credentials, I couldn't secure a job. It couldn't be the job market. At the time, the economy was doing great. Jobs were plentiful. It couldn't be my profile and resume. After all, I had all those materials prepared by the best career services from a top 20 computer science university and there was no reason a hiring manager would reject my resume. The answer had to lie within me.

So, what I did next was to spend the next few months studying what made top notch executives do well in life. I studied careers of folks who became CEOs of organizations, COOs of organizations, GMs of organizations, VPs and Directors of organizations and learned what made these overachievers tick. Why was it the case that there were some people who had "jobs" and some others who had "careers"? I tried to figure out how did these folks get such amazing opportunities and what did it take to create a career path like theirs. Simply put, I was obsessed with their success and wanted to create a path for myself that mimicked them.

When I started getting answers, I realized that the answers were in fact very simple and it was I who was overcomplicating the entire process. The answers to truly ace an interview and get a dream job offer lay in focusing on simple concepts that proved one and only one thing to your future employer – "What value can I add to your organization and if you can add value to my organization is it enough to offset what I pay you?"

I started applying these learnings to my own life and today the rest is history. From a job offer at Microsoft, the largest software company in the world, to Bridgewater Associates, the largest hedge fund in the world, to

Groupon, the fastest growing startup in the world, to Amazon, the world's biggest online retailer, I've seen it all. I have served in the position of Vice President, Director, Chief Operating Officer, Chief Executive Office running teams of between five and fifty across every functional area and in over 10 countries. Once again, I do not state these to you to impress upon you my credentials, but simply to show you that I know what I'm talking about and can help you take your career from "average" to the "next level".

However, the reason I write this book is beyond my personal experience as an interviewee. The bigger revelation came when interviewing candidates. In short, most people out there have no idea how to interview correctly. 90% of the candidates walking into my door were so terrible at interviewing that one must wonder why would they even spend time applying and going through the interview process.

The concepts that I had applied to my life, the same concepts used by six and seven figure executives to take their careers to the "next level", were far from being applied by today's candidate. So much so that I feel compelled to put all my thoughts down on paper.

That's exactly what my mission is with this book. It is a step-by-step guide to help you ace your upcoming interview. It's a 360-degree experience to ensure that you absolutely put all the pieces together to win the game of interviewing. It is fifteen years of trial and error on my path both as an interviewer and an interviewee. It has learnings from six and seven figure executives' careers and, in my opinion, is a complete blueprint to ace your upcoming interview.

No, this guide is not a comprehensive guide to answer every question in an interview. That, in my opinion, is only a small piece of the interview process. This guide is a step-by-step process to take you from the initial application for your job interview to a job offer.

The book has a certain approach to it. I will use a combination of both theory and practice as an approach to helping you succeed. I will teach you a chapter and then I will give you homework to complete. Your job is very simple: To read the chapter and then to do to homework. One more thing you've got to do: Do your homework. Oh, and one more: Don't forget to do your homework. I might have forgotten to mention that you need to do your homework. I think you're getting my point. Use this guide just like you are sitting in a classroom and someone is taking you one chapter at a time through a textbook and asking you to do homework at the end of it.

Trust me the effort will pay off. Now let's get started.

Introduction – The 5 x 3 Dream Career Blueprint

Great, you are still here. I'm so very excited that you've decided to join me for the rest of this journey. I hope my story and background has inspired you to continue reading and I've given you enough of a background for you to listen to me.

Let me start then by giving you my general approach to everything I do in life. When I decide to do something, I go for it. I lay out a plan. Then, I execute on my plan. I don't look left or right when I'm executing. I'm singularly focused on executing my plan keeping all the stupid people and distractions out of the way. At times, this is extremely difficult. After all, we do live in a very noisy social media world. However, I take the effort each day to recognize these distractions and do my best to overcome them. Nothing stops me from getting the outcome I've set out to achieve. This approach of putting down a plan together and focused execution of the plan is what has enabled me to push forward in life. Execution has been the linchpin to everything that I do.

My only request for you while you are reading this book is to do the same thing. I've spent all the time to lay out the plan for you. I can show you the path, I can show you the way, but only you can decide whether you want the outcome or not. You must decide whether you are going to go all in and execute on the plan or you are going to casually read this book and put it down somewhere and come back to it later in life. If you don't want the outcome, put this down right now. But if you want the outcome and are willing to follow others who have done this before, then continue to read on.

I'm going to be honest with you that it's not going to be easy. The path I've laid out for you is going to be tough. You are going to see rejection. You are going to see failure. But you must fight everything that comes in your way, get your mental strength up and execute. Know that I'm there with you every step of the way to help you, motivate you and keep you on track.

So, with that being said, let's get exactly into that – your plan. In Figure 1, I've laid out a complete blueprint for your career. It's called "ACCELERATE - The 5 x 3 Dream Career Blueprint". Print is out, stick it on the fridge, do whatever you can to make sure this is in front of you regularly for the rest of your life. This is a blueprint followed by me as I've gone through my career. This is the blueprint followed by six and seven figure executives that have enabled them to get to where they are in life today. Now, this is YOUR career blueprint. This blueprint is a step-by-step plan in excruciating detail that will take your career from "average" to "the next level".

This blueprint is the foundation for your entire career. The blueprint consists of five core steps and three acceleration steps. The next two chapters of this section will summarize YOUR career blueprint in detail. Then the rest of the book will go through step-by-step through step 3, which is about mastering the interview mastery blueprint. Your job is to follow each step of the blueprint. Like we've mentioned before, with each step comes homework for you to do. Your job is "To Do". Just consistently follow along, do the homework and a dream career with a dream salary is waiting for you just around the corner. Now GO...

Chapter 1 – The 5 Core Steps

Overview

Most students and professionals don't think of their careers in terms of a blueprint. Instead they equate careers to "having a good job". Yes, your job is part of your career, but it not the only part of your career. Instead, I'd like to present in this chapter an alternative definition of thinking about your career. I'd like to present to you "ACCELERATE – The 5 x 3 Dream Career Blueprint" that consists of five core steps and three acceleration steps. In this chapter, we will cover the five core steps and then in chapter 2 we will discuss how to accelerate your results three times using three acceleration steps.

The five core steps are all jotting down your long-term goals and putting a plan in place to achieve them. It is also about smaller plans to execute and achieve your long-term goals. But just applying the five core steps are not enough. To truly accelerate your career, there are three additional steps that need to be applied consistently. Applying these three steps consistently through the process will ensure that you see absolute acceleration of your results.

Figure 1 summarizes the entire process in detail.

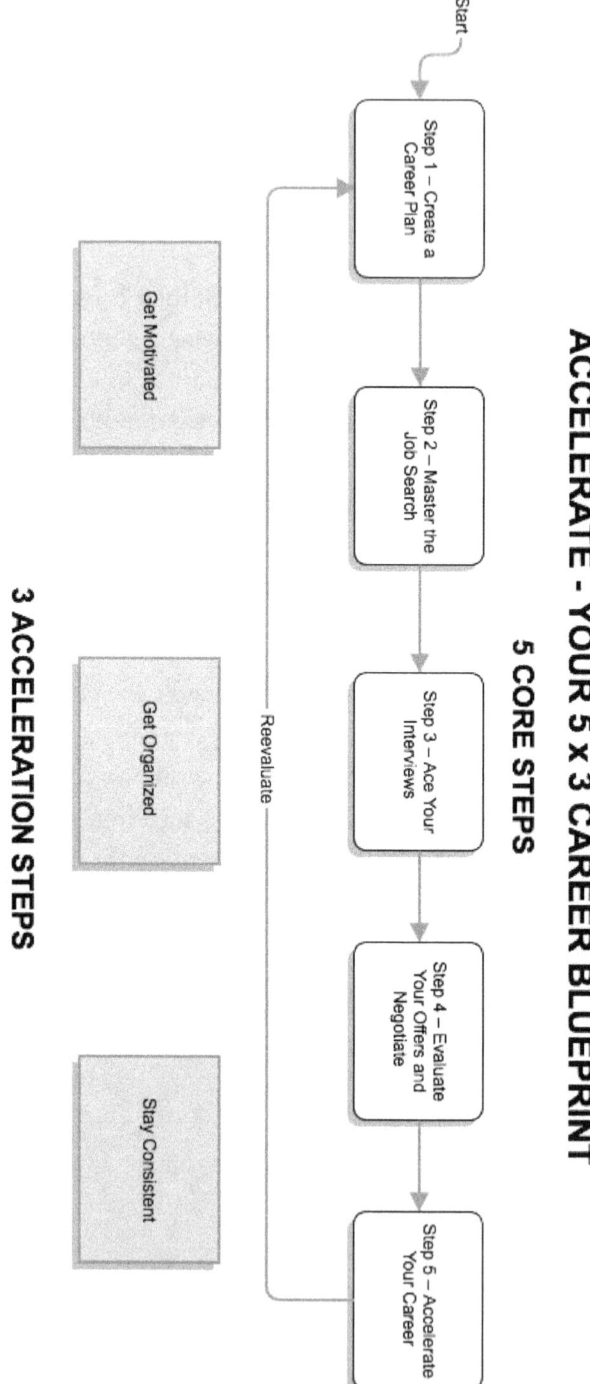

Figure 1 – The 5 x 3 Dream Career Blueprint

The 5 Core Steps

Step 1 – Create a Career Plan

I'd like for you to imagine for a second that you are an organization or a company and not an individual. Think about how companies operate for a second. Companies don't proceed with the execution of their business without a clear strategic plan. Executives spend tons of time, before a fiscal year, defining the company's vision, mission, values, and then defining a strategy to compete in their target market. From this strategy flows an operational plan to execute on the strategy and to get results. Through the year and over the next few years, executives and teams work hard to execute on that strategic plan and achieve company goals. However, companies don't just stop there. They constantly review how they are doing as part of achieving their goals. They consistently take a pulse on the status of that plan – irrespective of whether they achieved their planned goals or not. If they achieved their goals, then next year, companies will set even more aggressive goals. If they didn't achieve their goals, then will relook at what went wrong and fix their plan as necessary.

The point: Companies don't execute until they have a strategy in place.

Now, bring yourself back to YOU. If we keep the same analogy in place, there should be no reason that professionals execute on their career without a clear strategy in place. There should be no reason that individuals not take a pulse on their plan regularly and adjust or set aggressive goals each year. Yes, even for their careers.

This strategy needs to be defined as part of your career plan, like the strategic plan that organizations kick the year off with. Unfortunately, most people look for jobs. This is equivalent to a company going ahead and executing on a day to day basis, without a strategy in place and without a direction in which they want to go. Imagine how disruptive that would be to an organization.

This is step 1 – Create a Career Plan. The goal of the career plan is to define your values as an individual, your vision (or long-term goal for your life) and your mission to get closer towards your vision (the plan to execute on your vision).

When you don't go through this process, you land up taking up a job that you don't love, or you work for the paycheck or you don't get paid what your worth or you're not satisfied with the difference you are making in this world etc. etc. instead of truly creating a career for yourself that is meaningful, rewarding and fulfilling. The result – wasted human capital, wasted monetary capital, wasted time, and wasted opportunities to gain long term wealth.

Instead, step back, focus on the big picture first and use that to take your career to the next level. Conclusion: Start with step 1 – Put your career plan together before proceeding with your next job.

Appendix A has details on the entire career planning blueprint.

Step 2 – Master the Job Search

The outcome of step 1 will be of the following: A long term career plan (based on your values, your dream life etc. etc.) and a short term next move that you need to make to get there. Your next move consists of: The job title, the position, the industry, and location that you are going to target as part of your job search. This doesn't have to be a new company. It could just mean a promotion in your current role or a new department within your current company. It could also mean going back to school to get another job.

This is the first step towards operating on your strategy. You are now executing. Finding that next job is next. Unfortunately, most people search for jobs incorrectly. They fall for the classic mistake in the book of applying on a company's website or on job boards. Those techniques don't work. Period. 80% of jobs are filled through something known as the "hidden job market". If you're new to this term and are surprised, don't worry about it. We'll be covering it in detail. Six and seven figure executives only tap into this hidden job market. Your ability to tap into this hidden job market is the key to success in the job search world. Executives know what this hidden job market is and take full advantage of the same.

Secondly, candidates create generic resumes and cover letters that are used to apply to tons of jobs. This process simply doesn't work. Hiring managers are scanning tons of resumes daily and unless they find a pretty close match to what they want, there is a low chance that they are going to get back to you. You've got to stand out from the crowd. Instead, think of creating a resume or curriculum vitae (CV) that is targeted to your ideal next job. Also, instead of thinking in terms of cover letters, think in terms of "Value Proposition Letters", that indicate to employers what value you can add to their teams. Again, if you have no idea what this is – don't sweat it. We'll get there.

Thirdly, candidates work directly with Human Resources (HR) of their target company. Another big mistake. The job of HR is simply to support the hiring team in the process, by filtering out resumes that don't match the job criteria. They can say NO to you, but they can't say YES. In fact, most HR folks don't even know what hiring managers are looking for. Instead focus on going after the hiring managers or other decision makers. Your goal as part of the job search process is to connect and build a relationship with your hiring manager, get your profile in front of them and showcase the value you can bring to them and their teams

Another issue is the lack of "Thought Leadership" that today's candidates showcase. In today's competitive job search world, you will need to stand out and provide "Thought Leadership" on what you can offer to prospective employers. This one technique, again used by six and seven figure executives is crucial to differentiating yourself from the crowd, so that employers already know what you can bring to be table as they are researching you in today's social world.

Finally, you need retrain your mind to think of yourself as a "Product" and a complete package that is to be presented to employers. This package includes your resume, value proposition letter (VPL) and your thought leadership. The resume and VPL is the "Product" that a company would offer to its customers. The "Thought Leadership" is like marketing and brand building that companies will do to attract customers. Just like a company, you are attracting companies to your company a.k.a. YOU.

Appendix B has details on the job search mastery blueprint.

Step 3 – Ace Your Interviews

The outcome of step 2 is nothing but several job interviews in your desired job position, title, industry, and location all defined as part of your career plan. Next comes the phase of acing those interviews. Highly talented candidates lose out on opportunities due to their lack of preparation when it comes to interviews. As mentioned before, today's job market is highly competitive. With technology, has come the ability for companies to easily outsource their work. Making a fulltime hire is a big decision for the company and so they are being extremely selective. That's why you need to walk into your job search with utmost confidence and answer every question with ease.

How does this happen?

Simple: you need to put yourself into the shoes of the company and truly understand what they are looking for. Then you've got to prepare. You've got to prepare hard. This sounds simple in theory, but many professionals don't spend the time doing this before their job interviews. The outcome, lost opportunities.

The big takeaway from this step is to focus on preparing well for your upcoming job interview and truly understand what this company cares for aka their problems. Then present yourself as a solution to their problems. Do it by thoroughly researching the market, the company, the interview process. Do it by studying and practicing. Do it by asking the right questions. Do it by. preparing yourself well for interview day.

This entire book focuses on this step – to absolutely nail your upcoming interview.

Step 4 – Evaluate Your Offers and Negotiate

The outcome of step 3 (hopefully) is many job offers. This is a great outcome and many of you should be proud to be there. But your job is not over yet. To ensure that you enjoy the benefits of a successful long-term career and do what you love, you must objectively evaluate your job offers and pick a company that matches your values we defined in step 1, when we created your career plan. That was the whole point of it, right?

Once you pick a job you want to go with, you'll need to think about the offer and whether negotiation makes sense. Most professionals don't negotiate their offers. Why not? You should take the time to think deeply about their offer, evaluate the offer to your career plans and negotiate as necessary in the right fashion and with confidence. At the end of the day, you need to make sure that you get paid what you are worth and this is exactly what this step is about.

Step 4 will be covered in detail in Appendix C.

Step 5 – Accelerate Your Career/Get Promoted

So, you've picked a job after your evaluation process, negotiated the offer and everything was accepted for both sides. You're happy that this job and offer is getting you closer to your long term as outlined in step 1. Congratulations. This is the time to take it easy and breathe a little.

But don't get too complacent. We've got to work to do.

Step 5 is an extremely crucial step. The first 90 to 180 days in any company are going to establish you as a leader in the organization and position yourself for long term success. This is equivalent to the "under commit and over deliver" concept that you've probably heard off. When you join a company, the company doesn't know what you can offer, outside of the interview process. It's your job to prove to them that you mean business, that you can deliver. You want them to start trusting you and put you into the "Insider Circle". The first 90 to 180 days will define that.

Most people think that getting promoted is outside of their hands. I beg to differ. I truly believe that if you have a strong plan in place and the discipline to execute, you can position yourself for a promotion.

In fact, this is done using a 3-step framework: 1. By doing great work 2. By consistently promoting yourself and 3. By networking internally and externally.

The outcome – faster career growth compared to any of your peers. We'll see details on how to put together and execute on a promotion plan in Appendix D.

Repeat

The final step in our process is "Repeat". This is where the magic comes into play. Most professionals go through their careers in jobs that they do not evaluate yearly. This is equivalent to a company going through their execution each year without taking a pulse on how they are doing and what makes sense to do over the next year. There is a reason why we hear all about Microsoft's and Google's results in the news and what their plans for the next year are. The point is that organizations take a pulse each year on how they did and what their plans are for the next year.

That's exactly what top executives do each year and what professionals should do.

Each year you need to ask yourself this one question:

"Will what I do over the next year take me closer to my long-term goals?"

If the answer is yes, proceed with where you are. If not, you've got to go through the entire process once again. This means move departments, look for another job, go back to school. Do something that will get your closer to your long term and commit to it whole heartedly towards your long term.

That's exactly how progress is made fast. When you take a pulse regularly on where you are and adjust depending on how closer or further away you are from your long-term goals, you won't even realize how close you will be towards your vision.

Chapter 2 – The 3 Acceleration Steps

So far, I've shown you the 5 core steps that you should do regularly every year. If you do so, I have no doubt that you will see your career accelerate in no time and will position you for long term career success and wealth.

The biggest issue that most people face as they go through the entire process is that they give up too soon. I've laid out an entire plan for you, however, I never said that it was easy. If it were that easy everyone would be the VP, Director, or an executive in their company. The truth is that only a few get there. Why? Because of their ability to overcome any rejection along the way. Because of their ability to get organized. Because of their ability to come back to the ring every day. That's exactly what I'll cover in the 3 acceleration steps.

The 3 Acceleration Steps

Six and seven figure executives know that the process to getting to the top is not going to be easy. There are going to be pitfalls along the way that they must overcome.

These 3 steps are all about ensuring that they don't sight of the vision. The 3 acceleration steps are:

Get Motivated

This step is all about getting your mind right through the process. It's all about setting you up for peak performance as you go through your 5 core steps and not giving up during downtimes. It's about looking at the entire career seeking process as a big game of numbers and attaching no emotions to the process. You've probably heard the old saying that executives are thick skinned. Good. Now it's time for you to be thick skinned, move all the stupid people out of your way and execute on your plan.

Get Organized

This step is all about getting organized. How are you tracking your career plan and progress? How are you keeping track of your target companies, your network, hiring managers etc. etc.? How are you following up them regularly? Is your calendar up to date? Are you scheduling time to network? Have you put together your 90-day plan? All this requires stellar prioritization and organization. That's exactly what this step is all about.

Stay Consistent

Finally, you've got to stay consistent. You've got to come back every day and slowly push yourself in the right direction. Just like a company expects its employees to come to work every day, you've got to come back to the game every single day and focus on YOU, your career, your brand, your job search, your interviews, your 90-180-day plan etc. etc. However bad things get, however long you've been out of a job, or a promotion, you've got to come back every day to the ring and give you absolute best.

These 3 steps if applied consistently on a day to day basis to the five core steps, I have no doubt will take your career from average to the next level.

In appendices E, F, and G, I have detailed notes on how you should start following the three acceleration steps right now and throughout your career.

Chapter 3 – The 8 x 3 Interview Mastery Blueprint

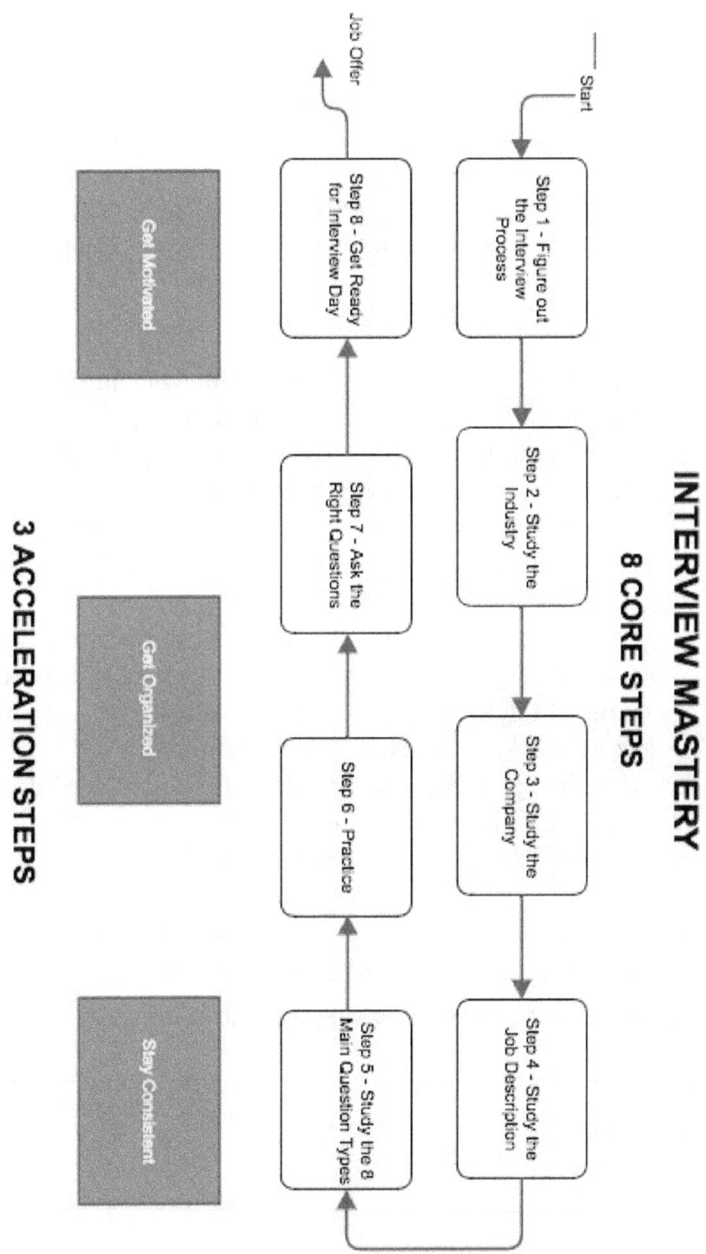

Figure 2 – The 8 x 3 Interview Mastery Framework

Now let's get into the meat of interviewing, which is the foundation of this book. My goal by the end of this book is ensure that you get your dream offer from your dream company.

To get your dream job at your target company, I believe that there are eight core steps that you need to follow, one step at a time.

In addition, I believe that you can significantly accelerate your results if you follow the 3 additional acceleration steps throughout the process.

The eight core steps are as follows:

1. Figure out the interview process at your target company for the position you are interviewing for.
2. Study your target company's industry in detail.
3. Study your target company in detail so that you are knowledgeable about everything regarding the company.
4. Study the job description for the position you are applying to in your target company.
5. Study the main question types. These question types are consistently asked as part of the interview at process at your target company. Then study the appropriate frameworks to answer these questions.
6. Practice, practice, and practice till you are confident.
7. Ask the right questions.
8. Get ready for interview day (I day).

The rest of the book will focus on these eight core steps. The three acceleration steps that we've covered before and in the appendices, will need to be followed as you are following the eight core steps.

Let's start with the eight core steps. Remember to do your homework at the end of each step.

Chapter 4 – Step 1 - Figure Out the Interview Process at your Target Company

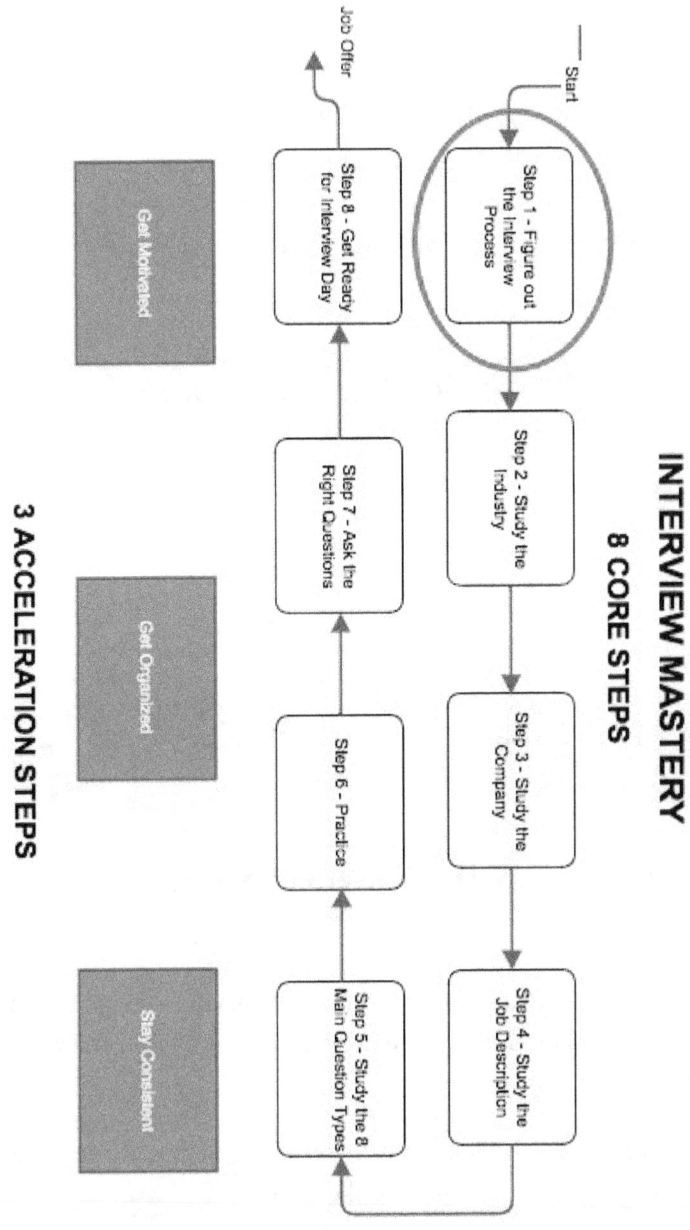

Figure 3 – The 8 x 3 Interview Mastery Framework – Step 1

Why Are We Doing This Step?

The reason we're doing this step is so that your expectations through the entire process are completely set. If the interview process at your target company consists of a presentation, then you better start preparing for a presentation. If the interview process at your target company consists of a group interview, well, then you better prepare for your group interview. The point is that the more crystal-clear on what you need to do, the more tailored you can prepare your interview preparation plan.

Typical Interview Process

A typical interview process for consists of the following:

---

3 Screens + Onsite Interview

First (Optional) Screen – Recruiter Screen

The first screen is with a recruiter who will walk you through the role, judge your general interest for the position and ask you some general questions on your background.

Sometimes recruiters will look at your resume and directly connect you with the hiring manager as the first phone screen.

They also judge which team would be a good fit for you based on your background, interests etc.

Their goal is to see whether it makes sense to pass you onto to the hiring manager for the next screen.

Most likely this is conducted on the phone, although sometimes you might meet recruiters on campus or at a career fair.

Second Screen – Hiring Manager or Team Member Screen - 30-60 minutes

This is the core of the interview and is the most important interview of your entire loop. The hiring manager is deciding in this interview whether you will be a good member of his or her team.

He or she is looking for 3 specific items – Strengths (can you do the job?), Motivation (why would you come to work every day?) And Fit (can the team tolerate working with you?)

We've covered all these types of questions in Steps 5 and 6 of this book.

Expect to be asked any of the question types that we're covered later in Chapter 5 in this interview.

You should be spending the bulk of your time preparing for this phone interview as it is the first critical gate to the entire interview. (Not to worry we've provided a study calendar later).

Third Screen (Optional) – Hiring Manager or Team Member Screen - 30-60 minutes

The third screen will either be like the second screen or the company might go deeper into certain areas of your resume.

Sometimes this screen is conducted as part of the recruiting process for the company. Sometimes it is conducted because the hiring manager couldn't get deeper into certain question types and is still unclear about your strengths, motivation and fit.

Whatever the case, best is to be prepared for this screen.

Onsite Interview

Once you get through these phone screens, the company will fly you over to their offices (or invite you if you are local) to conduct a thorough interview process.

Many a times this interview is conducted over video conferencing too, where you will meet many team members online.

Expect to go through five rounds of 45 minutes to an hour where you will be asked any of the question types in step 5.

Most likely one of the interviewers will be the hiring manager again. He or she will meet you again (after having spoken to you on the phone.)

Offer and Next Steps

You should know soon the decision of the hiring team - within a week or so after your interview. If you don't please email the hiring team politely and ask for a status update.

Different Types of Interviews

In addition to the overall interview pipeline, you will also encounter different types of interviews through the process. In this section, we've summarized the different types of interviews that you may encounter.

Some of these are newer formats that companies are resorting to these days.

1. **Phone Interview**

This is the most standard interview where the interviewer will call you during the agreed upon time.

2. **Video Conferencing Interview**

This is an extension of the phone interview. The only different being that you will be seeing your interviewer face to face on a video conference.

3. **1:1 In Person Interview**

This is a face to face interview where you and the interviewer will be sitting directly in front of each other.

4. **Group Interview**

This is an extension of the face to face interview where you will be part of the larger group of either multiple interviewers or interviewees. These come in two flavors.

   1. **One Interviewer and Many Interviewees**

In this interview, there will be multiple interviewees in a group setting and one interviewer conducting the interview.

2. **One Interviewee and Many Interviewers**

In this interview, there will be multiple interviewers trying to interview you during the same interview session.

5. **Lunch/Social Interview**

In this interview, you will be taken by the interviewer to a social setting such as coffee or lunch.

6. **Presentation Interview**

In this interview, you will be asked to present to a group of interviewers and you will be asked questions.

7. **Assignment Interview**

In this interview, you will be asked to do a case study or a project and submit that to the interviewing team. This could be timed or not.

8. **Test Interview**

In this interview, you will be asked to take a test (most likely online). You will proceed to the next stage of the interview pipeline based on the results of the test. This could be timed or not.

These different interview types vary from company to company. The entire interview pipeline is nothing but a mix and match of these different interview types.

Homework

Now, it's time to do your homework. Yes, I know this chapter was short and simple, but we're only getting started.

Find out what the overall interview pipeline is for the position of you are applying to at your target company and then write it down below. Get crystal-clear on the expectations of that process. Please add as much detail as possible here. The types of interview, the number of interviews, the expectations of each interview etc. etc. By the end of this homework, you should have no doubt and be crystal-clear about the interview process in your target company.

Stage 1:

____

Stage 2:

____

Stage 3:

____

Stage 4:

____

Stage 5:

____

Stage 6:

____

Stage 7:

____

Stage 8:

____

Stage 9:

____

Stage 10:

____

Stage 11:

____

Chapter 5 – Step 2 – Study the Industry

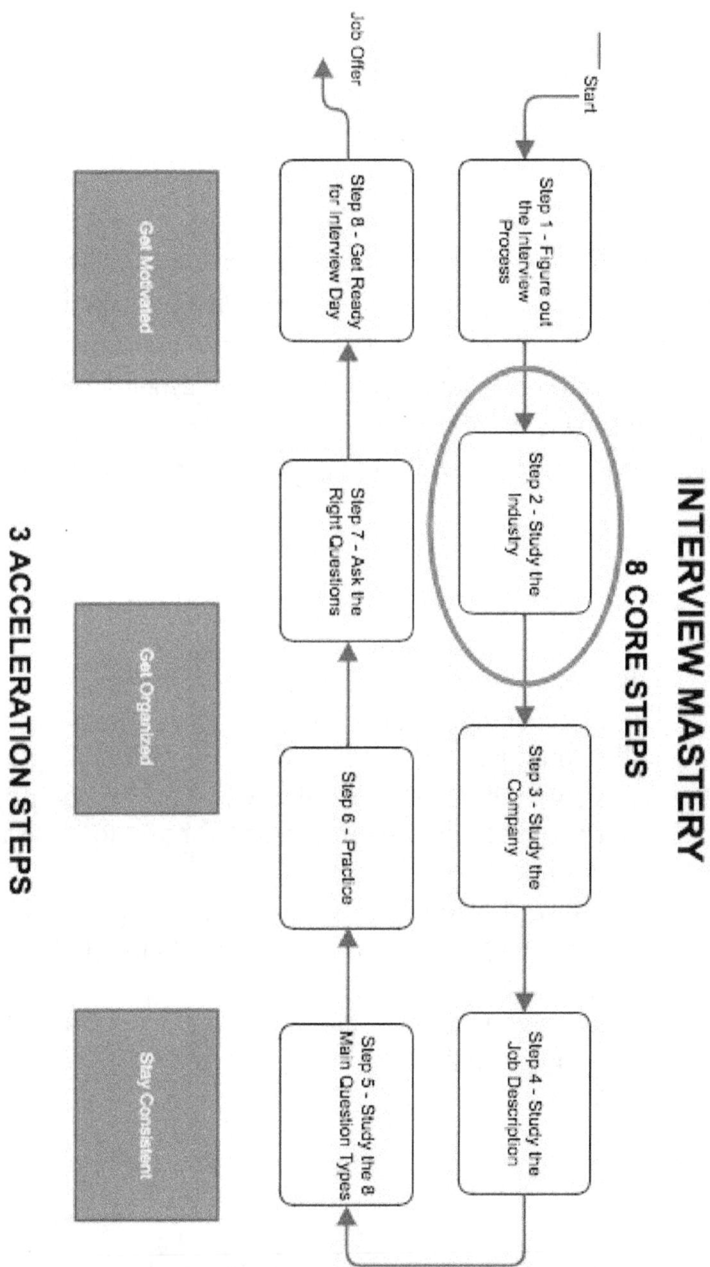

Figure 4 – The 8 x 3 Interview Mastery Framework – Step 2

Now that we're clear on the interview process for the position you are interviewing for in your target company, the next step is the study the industry that your company operates in detail.

Why Are We Doing This Step?

A lot of companies are now asking questions about your interest and knowledge of the industry that you are working in. So, the better prepared you are, the better you will stand apart from the crowd. However, irrespective of whether you are asked questions about the industry, your knowledge of the opportunities and challenges in the industry, will help you create a strong story during your interviews.

Additionally:

- Possibly you have been out of the industry for a while and you are now looking to get back in.
- Possibly you are a student and have been so involved in your academics that the job search is finally coming to the frontline.
- Possibly there has a rise of newer, smaller companies or startups that might be interesting for you to join that you didn't know about.
- Possibly the job market has different packages (base, bonus, salary) and you want to get a pulse on what's right for you.
- Perhaps you want to learn about the interview process in the companies in your industry.

Whatever the case, this step is important so that you are well prepared in your conversations.

So, with that little background let's jump straight into the information we should collect.

Identify Your Target Industry

The first thing to do is to identify the target industry that your company belongs to and operates in. The important point here is to try to be narrow about it.

For example: You might be a software engineer looking to work for a company like Sears, so your industry would be retail technology, not the general technology industry.

For example: You might be a consultant looking to work for a large consulting firm in their energy practice, so your target industry would be energy consulting.

Most likely you will have one main target industry, but it is not common to have two or three.

As you continue to study daily, you might find newer and interesting industries, so you can update this list too during your preparation and start applying to opportunities in those industries.

Then, for each industry study the following:

Details of Each Industry

1. How large is the industry?
2. What is the projected growth rate of the industry?
3. How is this industry segmented?
4. Who are the top 3-5 players in that industry?
5. Top opportunities for the industry.
6. Top challenges that the industry is facing.

Note that you don't need to answer every question in detail. Sometimes a question might not make sense. Use this as a template to kick start your thinking process.

Example:

Let's say that you're interested in in the role of a product manager and you want to join a startup in Silicon Valley.

In this case, it's simple that the obvious choice for target industry is the technology industry, but more importantly you want to hone in on the startup scene in Silicon Valley.

Industry	Technology Industry with a focus on startups.

Figure 5 – Choice of Industry

Next, we'll collect data on the technology industry in the valley. Here is an example of data you would collect.

How large is the industry?	The startup industry in Silicon Valley seems to be growing with tons of new capital coming in and tons of startups getting funded. The funding environment is strong. Investors seem to be wanting to put money into Virtual Reality startups. It seems like the hot trend in the valley right now.
What is the projected growth rate of the industry?	The growth rate seems strong and analysts are projecting continued growth for the tech sector over the next 2 years.
Who are the Top 3-5 players in that industry?	Not specific companies, but the top Venture Funds in the area seem to be: Sequoia capital, Andreessen Horowitz, Kleiner Perkins. I'd be interested in getting a job in one of their portfolio companies.

Figure 6 – Industry Details

Top opportunities for the industry.	From the perspective of the industry, there seems be tons of opportunity in the cloud. Lots of companies are moving to the cloud. Another opportunity seems in retail. Companies like Sears, Nordstrom are struggling with competitors like Amazon, so are looking to acquire smaller startups.
Top problems that the industry is facing.	Looks like the turnover in silicon valley is very high. Companies fire at ease and employees leave fast too. Sustainability seems to be an issue. Lots of companies in the valley are just looking for quick exits and not for long term growth.

Figure 7 – Industry Challenges and Opportunities

Identify Positions and Levels in the Industry

Next you should get clear on the positions in the industry.

The reason we do this is because tons of companies have different titles to represent the same job role. E.g. A Product Manager at Google is like a Program Manager at Microsoft and like Technical Program Manager at Amazon.

So, spend time understanding the different titles in the industry. This will help when finding and applying for jobs later.

Also, get clear on the different levels in the industry.

Different industries use different levels differently. A VP in financial services is very junior compared to a VP in the technology industry.

Some larger companies have many internal levels. E.g. Microsoft has the concept of 59, 60, 61. Amazon has levels 5, 6, 7. Getting clear on the levels used and where you would fit in early in the process again will help you have good conversations.

Identify Typical Pay Packages in The Industry

The next set of information you want to collect is typical salary information for your job title, level, and the industry.

Why?

Salary and other topics with come up during the conversations throughout the process, so you want to be prepared.

Typical components of salary would include: base salary, bonus, and equity

Get familiar with what are the typical pay packages at your level for the job title and industry you are targeting.

Identify the Typical Interview Process

Next you should dive deeper into the typical interview process in your industry and compare it to the typical interview process we discussed earlier.

This is useful as it helps eliminate any assumptions and you are well prepared to ace the interview.

Typical Interview Process in Silicon Valley for Product Managers	The process is pretty typical. Initial Phone Screen, followed by an onsite. However, most companies also make you do a case study and then ask you to present your work to a panel. I'll need to prepare for this case study and add time to google calendar.

Figure 8 – Typical Interview Process in the Industry

Why? When I'm already interviewing.

If you are already interviewing, you should already know about this process for your target company.

If you don't have any interviews yet, then you should start preparing for any areas that deviating from the norm.

For example: The "case study" in the product manager case.

Identify Companies You Are Interested In

Finally, start putting a list of the companies you are interested in your industry.

This is not a final list and as you do your research you should add to this list continuously.

But by now you should start getting a sense of the interesting players in the space that would potentially be part of your plan of your application process.

Why? When I'm already interviewing.

If you are already interviewing, this step is optional. If you don't have any interviews yet, then you should start putting together a target list of companies and then apply to each one of them. Additionally, even if you are interviewing, you can spread your risk by applying to more companies you come across during your research.

Conclusion

So, after this step, you should be well versed with your target company's industries and what's been happening there.

- You have a clearer idea about the details of those industries.
- You should know what the typical interview process is for those industries.
- You should know the typical titles in the industry.
- You should know the typical salary ranges in your industry for the level you are targeting.
- Additionally, you should have your list of companies that you are excited about, the ones that you are going to go after and apply to.

Homework

Please use the "Industry" worksheet and fill out details about the industry your company operates in. Use one sheet per industry that you want to analyze.

Industry Worksheet

1. Target Company Industry Details

Industry Name:

____

a. How large is the industry?

____

____

____

b. What is the projected growth rate of the industry?

____

____

____

c. How is the industry segmented?

____

____

____

d. Who are the top 3-5 players in that industry?

____

____

____

e. Top 3 opportunities for the industry.

____

____

f. Top 3 challenges that the industry is facing.

2. **Typical interview process in the industry**

3. **Typical positions and levels in the industry**

4. **Typical salary ranges for position and level in the industry**

5. **Initial list of target companies**

Chapter 6 – Step 3 – Study the Company

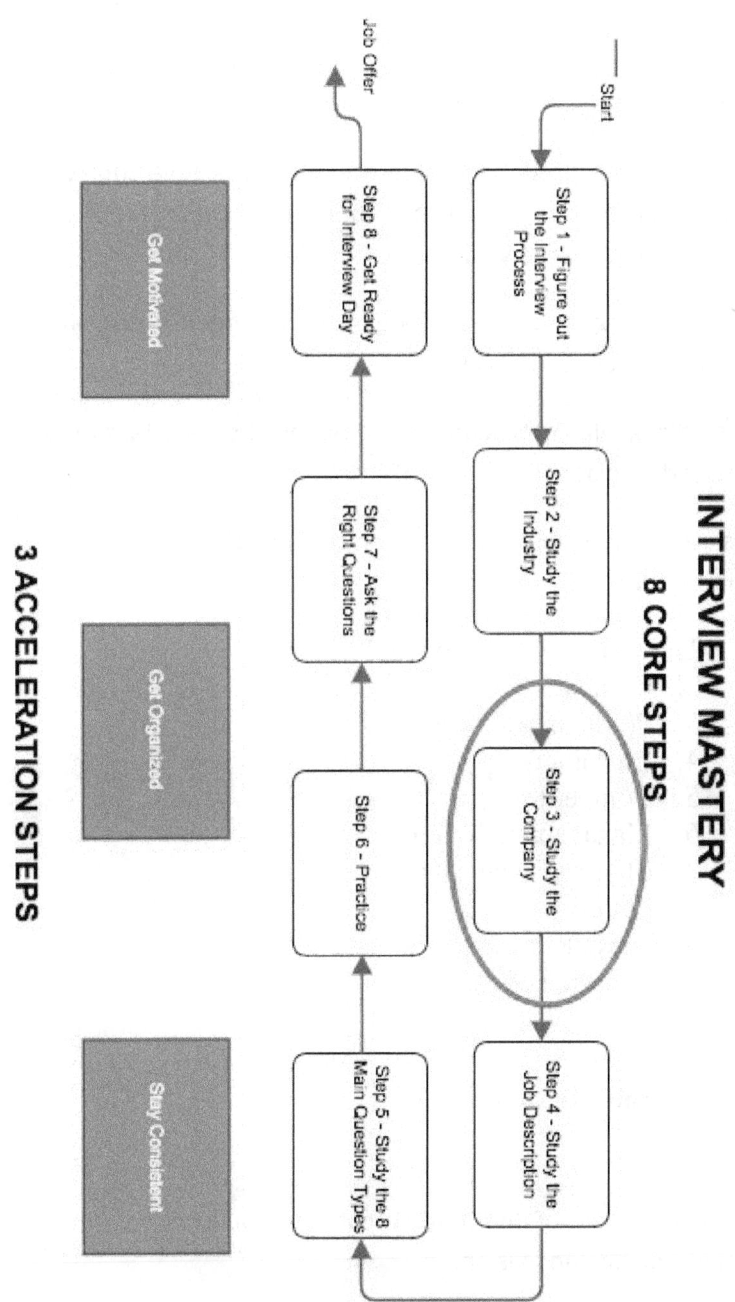

Figure 9 – The 8 x 3 Interview Mastery Framework – Step 3

Studying Your Company – A 10 Step Framework

If you have ever interviewed before, you should know that questions regarding the company are common throughout the process.

You want to show throughout the process that you have done your research about the company, know where the company is going and why you're excited about the same.

This chapter will give you a list of areas that you need to prepare for before going into the interview.

When studying information about a company, it's important for us to have a framework in place.

Here is a good framework to use when studying the company that you are interviewing with.

1. Company's Vision and Mission
2. Company's Culture and Values
3. Products and Services
4. Customers
5. Competitors
6. Management Team
7. Metrics/Financials
8. Future
9. News/Rumors
10. Interviewers

Vision and Mission

This is the first piece of information that you should collect – the company's mission and vision.

- A company's vision is nothing but its long-term dream.
- Its mission is the current task at hand to achieve that vision.

Some companies define mission as the purpose or the reason why they exist. Additionally, some companies define their mission and vision in a single statement.

Whatever the case, you should understand the vision for the company and its current mission.

Where do I find it?

You can easily find this information on the company's corporate site. Just do a google search for "<company name> vision" or "<company name> mission". Startups or smaller private may not have this information, so do your best to get what you can online.

Example: Google

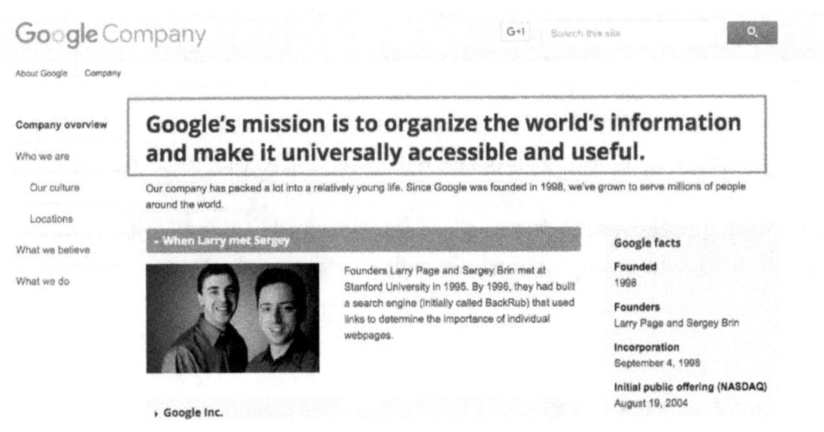

Figure 10 – Google's Mission and Vision

If you do a google search for "Google's mission and vision", you should be able to see a page like this that states that "Google's mission is to organize the world's information and make it universally accessible and useful".

Whatever company you are applying to, make sure you understand its vision and mission and internalize it before going into the interview process.

Culture and Values

Next is "Culture" and "Values".

- Culture is the processes and practices that make up the work environment.
- Values are the rules by which decisions are made on a day to day basis.

You will be an integral part of the culture, so it's important to internalize it and make sure that the culture of the company works for you. You will also get questions regarding the culture, so make sure that you're able to answer appropriately (more on this later).

Some companies have a tough culture, so you should do your research early on. Also, make sure you agree with the values of the company.

Again, do a google search for this information and internalize the culture and values before going into the interview.

Products and Services

Next, get a sense of the products and services that the company you are joining offers to its customers.

Be able to talk through one or two of the products in detail, so spend some time understanding them.

If you know which product you will be working with, make sure you understand that product.

Also, know 1 – 2 products you love about the company and why.

Additionally, 1 – 2 products that you dislike and would change. You don't need to be negative about it, but it will show the hiring team that you care enough about the company that you did detailed research on their products in advance.

Customers

Next are customers. At the end of the day, a business is in existence to acquire and retain customers. So, understanding them early on will give you an upper hand in the interview process.

A few questions to ponder over:

1. Who are the target customers for the company?
2. What's the demographic like? E.g. Single moms within the age of 25-35.
3. What do customers like about the company's products? What do they dislike?

Answers to these questions will surely tell the interviewers that you are well prepared for this role and you care about the customers of the company.

Competitors

If you go into your interview having a firm grasp of your target company's competitors and their differentiators, you will be well positioned to show your passion for this job.

Here is a list of questions you should answer:

1. List out 2-3 of the top competitors of the company.
2. Find out what do the competitors' do better than your target company.
3. What does the company do better than its competitors?

Again, a search for "<company>'s competitors" will give you a list.

Management Team

Find out who the CEO is. What is her or his background? The last thing you want is to get caught off guard on what the CEO's name is. Additionally, what does the rest of the management team consist of?

You will be working under the leadership of the senior management team – under their set-out mission, vision, values, and culture, so make sure you understand them and their style of operating.

Example: Amazon

The key man behind Amazon is Jeff Bezos. We recommend you read a brief bio on him – https://en.wikipedia.org/wiki/Jeff_Bezos. He runs a tight ship at Amazon, so you'll need to be familiar with his style of operating if you'd like to work there.

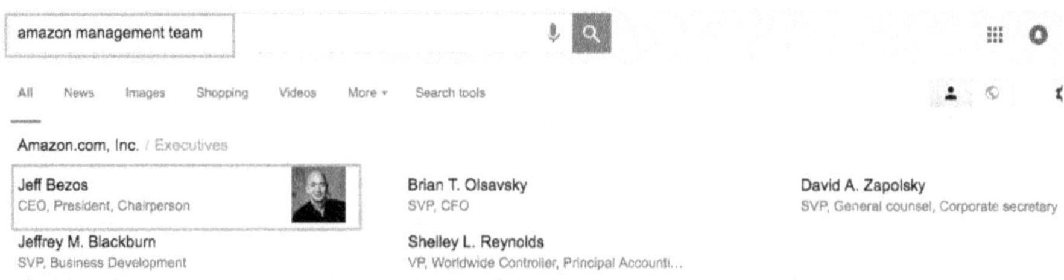

Figure 11 – Management Team

Metrics/Financials

Understand how the company did last year and last quarter.

1. You should find out its revenue, its gross profit, gross margin, net profit, and net margins.
2. You should find out how the business is growing; i.e. its growth rate.
3. You should find out which product is contributing to the most growth.

If your company is public, you should be able to find this information on finance.yahoo.com. It's harder if your company is private, so do your best. Employers will also understand if that is the case.

If the company is pre-revenue, try to find out other metrics like the total number of customers it has or its customer engagement metrics.

Opportunities/Future

Understand what the company wants to do in the future. What products/services does it want to introduce? Where does it want to invest in the future? What threats exist in achieving its future?

CEO's normally talk about their future in events, conferences and you should be able to find many YouTube videos on information like this.

Knowing this information and speaking about it during your interviews, will only show your passion for the company and your excitement towards joining them.

Rumors

For this section, I recommend pulling open the newspaper the morning of the interview and see what's going on with your company. Is there news of an acquisition? Maybe there's news about its earnings or growth or new offices its opening. Maybe there is a scoop that someone published. Whatever the case, be ready the day of the interview, so that you are not caught off-guard with any questions. At the same time, you'll be able to showcase your preparedness to the interviewer.

Interviewers

Start by finding out from your recruiter who your interviewers are.

Then go ahead to LinkedIn (or Google) and get a sense of who this person is, what their background is, which company do they come from. Anything that would be of interest to grab their attention.

Then during your interview, throw in 1-2 times something common about you and the interviewer.

For example: If you both worked at a prior company, you can always state that. If you have common connections on LinkedIn, you could state that. If there is some news about a prior or current company with the interviewer, state that. etc. etc.

Homework

As part of your homework and the information in this chapter, please go ahead and fill the "Company" worksheet and use that during your interview process.

Company Worksheet

1. **Company Name: ________________**

Vision, Mission, Culture, and Values

2. **Vision:**

____

____

3. **Mission:**

____

____

4. **Culture:**

____

____

5. **Values:**

____

____

Products/Services

6. **List of Products/Services:**

7. **Your favorite products and why?**

8. **Products you would change and why?**

Customers

9. **Target Customer**

10. Target Customer Demographics

11. What do customers like about the Products/Services?

12. What do customers dislike about the Products/Services?

Competitors

13. Main Competitors

14. What do Competitors' do better than Company?

15. What does Company do better than Competitors?

Management

16. Management Team (CEO, COO etc.)

Metrics

17. Financials/Metrics

a. **Revenue this and last year:**

---

b. **Gross Profit this and last year:**

---

c. **Gross Margins this and last year:**

---

d. **Net Profit this and last year:**

---

e. **Net Margins this and last year:**

---

f. **Growth Rate:**

---

g. **Which products/services contribute to the most growth?**

---

h. **Any other metrics e.g. Active Users**

Future

18. Company's Future Growth Plans (Where are they investing?)

News/Rumors

19. Recent News/Rumors

Notes

Interviewers

Name of the Interviewer

____

Discussion Topic with them

____

____

____

____

____

Name of the Interviewer

____

Discussion Topic with them

____

____

____

____

____

Name of the Interviewer

____

Discussion Topic with them

____

____

____

____

____

Interviewers

Name of the Interviewer

____

Discussion Topic with them

____

____

____

____

____

Name of the Interviewer

____

Discussion Topic with them

____

____

____

____

____

Name of the Interviewer

____

Discussion Topic with them

____

____

____

____

____

Chapter 7 – Step 4 – Study the Job Description

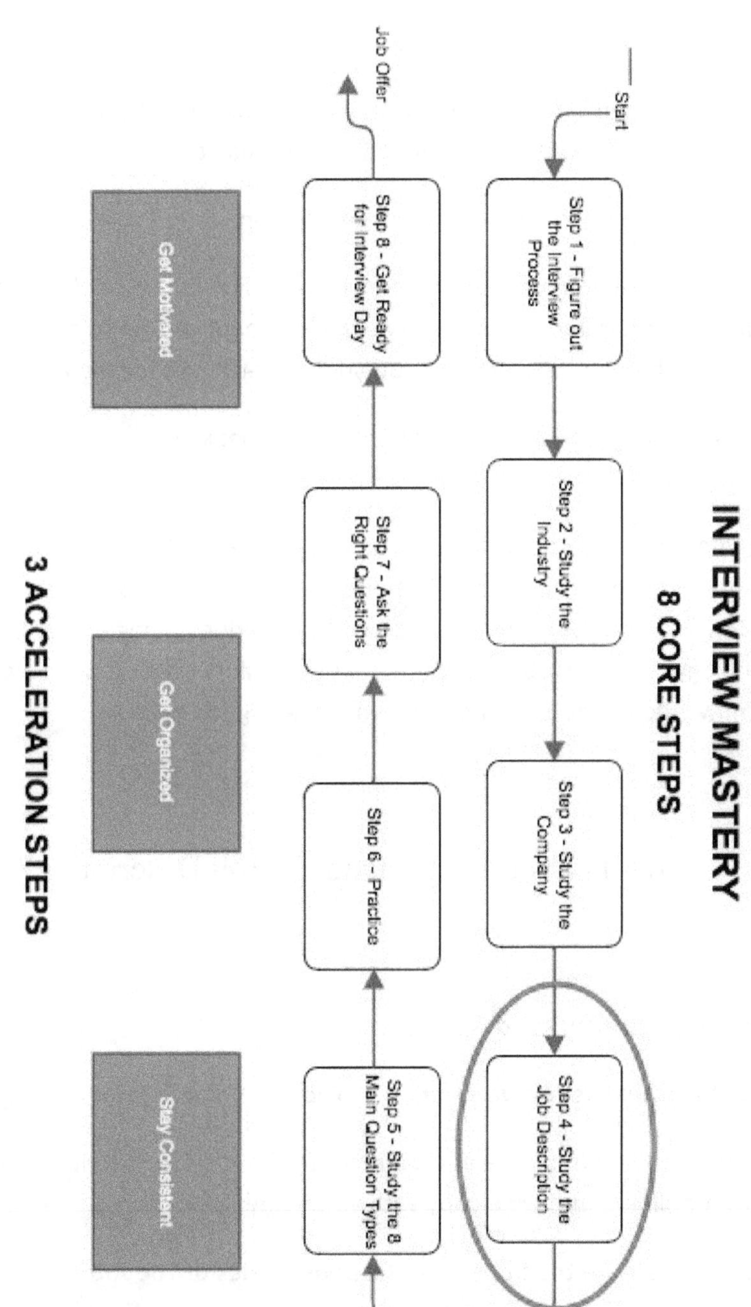

Figure 12 – The 8 x 3 Interview Mastery Framework – Step 4

Don't Ignore the Job Description

Interviewees often ignore the job description thinking that they know what the job is all about, especially after they speak to a recruiter.

My suggestion is to not ignore the job description

Think about it – if you can take the items line by line in the job description and speak about it during your interview, you would've convinced recruiters or hiring managers that you are the perfect fit for the job.

Speaking the language of the job description is speaking the language of the company.

Not to mention, think about who writes the job description. Yes, you guessed it – the hiring manager. Imagine that as you go through the interview process, every conversation with the hiring manager uses terminology from the job description that he or she wrote. You should well know who might be in the hiring manager's good books.

How Do You Understand the Job Description?

Here are my recommended steps...

Step 1: Print Out the Job Description of The Job You Are Interviewing For

If you don't have this, please ask the recruiter for the job description, or look for it online. But have a copy with you ready.

Step 2: Highlight All the Important Responsibilities of The Job

You can either mark this in the printed-out Job Description or start copy pasting the important responsibilities into another document for you to use later.

Example: Customer Service

Here is a typical customer service representative job description that we've taken from a job board on the internet.

Responsibilities

- Manage large amounts of incoming calls
- Generate sales leads
- Identify and assess customers' needs to achieve satisfaction
- Build sustainable relationships of trust through open and interactive communication
- Provide accurate, valid and complete information by using the right methods/tools
- Meet personal/customer service team sales targets and call handling quotas
- Handle complaints, provide appropriate solutions and alternatives within the time limits; follow up to ensure resolution
- Keep records of customer interactions, process customer accounts and file documents
- Follow communication procedures, guidelines and policies
- Take the extra mile to engage customers

Requirements

- Proven customer support experience or experience as a client service representative
- Track record of over-achieving quota
- Strong phone contact handling skills and active listening
- Familiarity with CRM systems and practices
- Customer orientation and ability to adapt/respond to different types of characters
- Excellent communication and presentation skills
- Ability to multi-task, prioritise, and manage time effectively
- High school degree

Figure 13 – Sample Customer Service Job Description

Next, let's highlight a few key points.

Responsibilities

- Manage large amounts of incoming calls
- Generate sales leads
- Identify and assess customers' needs to achieve satisfaction
- Build sustainable relationships of trust through open and interactive communication
- Provide accurate, valid and complete information by using the right methods/tools
- Meet personal/customer service team sales targets and call handling quotas
- Handle complaints, provide appropriate solutions and alternatives within the time limits; follow up to ensure resolution
- Keep records of customer interactions, process customer accounts and file documents
- Follow communication procedures, guidelines and policies
- Take the extra mile to engage customers

Requirements

- Proven customer support experience or experience as a client service representative
- Track record of over-achieving quota
- Strong phone contact handling skills and active listening
- Familiarity with CRM systems and practices
- Customer orientation and ability to adapt/respond to different types of characters
- Excellent communication and presentation skills
- Ability to multi-task, prioritize, and manage time effectively
- High school degree

Figure 14 – Key Responsibilities from Job Description

Step 3: For Each Responsibility, Think About Examples in Your Past Where You Have Showcased That Work

This is exactly why I've asked you to highlight these key points. There is a 100% chance that the questions you get during your interview process are going to test you on these specific skills mentioned in the job description.

So, if you prepare in advance good examples of how you've showcased that work and how it will translate to your new company, there is absolutely no reason you shouldn't ace the interview process and impress your interviewers.

Think of this as a cheat sheet for your interviews.

In our example with the job description we've provided:

You should:

- Have examples of where you've managed many incoming calls.
- Have examples of cases where you generated sales leads.
- Have examples of where you assessed customers' needs.
- Have examples of when you handled complaints.
- Have examples of when you had to multi-task, prioritize, and manage time effectively.

Etc. etc. etc. You get the point....

How Do You Prepare These Examples?

Don't worry we'll see these later when we discuss the main question types. For now, prepare your list and start thinking about good examples. Just prepare a list.

What If You Don't Have One the Requirements?

If it's one or two requirements that you are missing, then you may be fine:

In your interviews, if asked about that requirement you can use one of the following answers:

For Example: Say You Don't Have Any Experience Generating Sales Leads.

"I'm currently learning the process of generating sales leads through mentoring by another customer service manager. By the time I join the job, I'll be well prepared to apply my learnings to the job."

Or

"I understand that I don't have that specific skill, but I'm a fast learner and I don't suspect it will take me time to pick it up once I start. The skills I bring are clearly transferrable to this job."

However, if you are missing most of the requirements in the job description, you should question whether this is the right job for you and for you to spend so much time on.

Homework

Now it's time for action. It's time for your first homework, so let's get going. Here are the steps.

1. Print out the Job Description for the company you are interviewing with.
2. Highlight key requirements of the job from the Job Description.
3. Internalize the language used in the Job Description.
4. For each highlighted responsibility in the Job Description, please think about examples in the past where you have showcased those skills.

Use the "Job Description" worksheet to fill this in. Keep this handy during your phone interviews.

We will use these later in Step 5, as we go through practice questions to ensure that you're well prepared for the interview.

Job Description Worksheet

Key Responsibility from Job Description	Example

If you don't have examples for certain areas of the job description, then please write down responses to answers if you are asked.

Key Responsibility from Job Description that I don't have any experience in

____

Response:

____

____

____

____

____

Key Responsibility from Job Description that I don't have any experience in

____

Response:

____

____

____

____

____

Key Responsibility from Job Description that I don't have any experience in

____

Response:

____

____

____

____

Chapter 8 – Step 5 – Study the Main Question Types

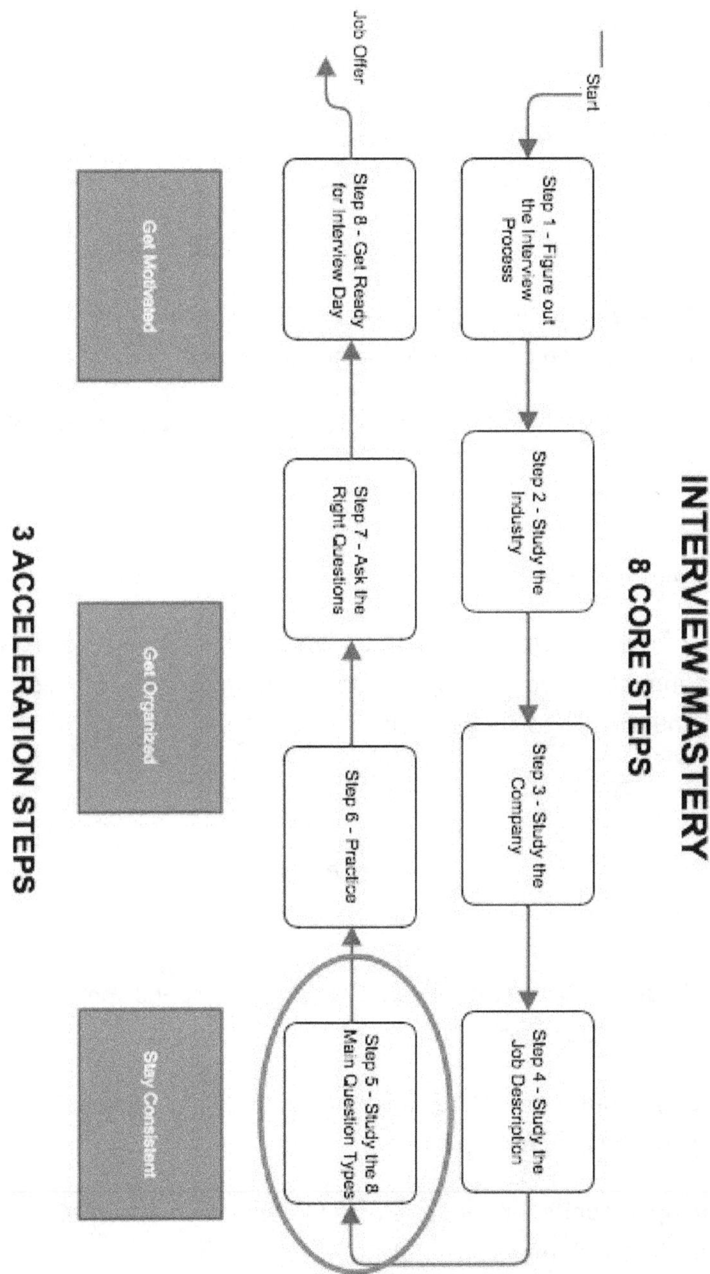

Figure 15 – The 8 x 3 Interview Mastery Framework – Step 5

YOU

Like we've discussed before, the success or failure of your interviews will hinge on your ability to clearly define who you are, what you know, and what you can do.

Remember our salesman analogy – you must keep talking about your unique product and features through the process.

You must showcase your strengths, motivations and fit.

Most candidates cannot talk about themselves, specifically when asked about an open-ended question. Most candidates just cannot sell.

Worst case is when they start discussing memorized answers in their interview.

In this section, you will focus on the process of knowing YOU before you start answering questions.

The goal of this section is for you to understand YOU. I want you to start thinking about YOU, your skills, your strengths and all the points of your life that you can use to sell yourself.

Homework

Please fill out the "YOU" worksheet. We'd like you spend some time answering every question.

Don't worry about specific language or the specific job description or anything, just be yourself here.

This is an opportunity for you to take the time and reflect on YOU. So, do take your time with these questions.

"YOU" Work Sheet

Work Experience

List down each of your jobs you've held in your entire career, even summer jobs, internships and volunteering experiencing.

Then for each employer list down:

1. Name, address, telephone number, and email address.
2. The names of all your supervisors and, whenever possible, where they can be reached.
3. Letters of recommendations (especially if they can't be reached)
4. The exact dates (month and year) you were employed.

For each job, include:

1. Specific duties and responsibilities.
2. Supervisory experience, noting the number of people you managed.
3. Specific skills required for the job.
4. Key accomplishments.
5. Dates you received promotions.
6. Any awards, honors, or special recognition you received.

Volunteer and Internship Experience

For each organization, you interned or volunteered at

1. Name, address, telephone number, and email address.

2. Name of your supervisor or the director of the organization.
3. Letter(s) of recommendation.
4. Exact dates (month and year) of your involvement with the organization.

For each volunteer experience or internship, include:

1. Approximate number of hours devoted to the activity each month.
2. Specific duties and responsibilities.
3. Skills required.
4. Major accomplishments.
5. Awards, honors, or special recognition you received.

Educational Achievements

For each school, you've attended:

1. Name
2. Address
3. Phone number
4. Years attended
5. Major area of study
6. Important (or relevant courses)
7. Honors
8. GPA
9. Class rank
10. Which courses you enjoyed the lost
11. Which courses you enjoyed the least
12. Which were your strongest subjects
13. Which were your weakest.

Other Activities, Honors, and Skills

List out all sports, clubs, and other activities you've participated, inside and outside school.

For each activity, club, or group:

1. Name and purpose.
2. Offices you held; special committees you formed, chaired, or participated in; or specific positions you played.
3. Duties and responsibilities of each role.
4. Key accomplishments.
5. Awards or honors you received.

Veterans

1. Final rank awarded.
2. Duties and responsibilities.
3. Citations and awards.
4. Details on specific training and/or any special schooling.
5. Special skills developed.
6. Key accomplishments.

You as a Person

1. Who are you? Describe your personality.
2. What are your values? What is important to you?
3. Which achievements did you enjoy the most? Which are you proudest of? Be ready to tell the interviewer how these accomplishments relate to the position at hand.
4. What in your personal life causes you the most stress (relationships, money, time constraints, and so on)? What gives you the most pleasure?
5. What mistakes have you made? Why did they occur? What have you learned from them? What have you done to keep similar things from occurring again?

6. How well do you interact with authority figures – bosses, teachers, parents? Be ready to furnish specific examples.
7. What are your favorite games and sports? Are you overly competitive? Do you give up too easily? Are you a good loser or a bad winner? Do you rise to a challenge or back away from it?
8. What kinds of people are your friends? Do you associate only with people who are like you? Do you enjoy differences in others – or merely tolerate them? What are some things have caused you to end friendships? What does this say about you?
9. If I were to ask a group of friends and acquaintances to describe you, what adjectives would they use? List all of them – the good and the bad. Why would people describe you this way? Are there specific behaviors, skills, achievements, or failures that seem to identify you in the eye of others? What are they?

You as a Professional

1. What kinds of people do you like working with? What kinds do you dislike working with?
2. What are your goals and aspirations?
3. What would it take to transform yourself into someone who's passionate about everyday workday?
4. What are your passions?
5. How can you make yourself more marketable in today's competitive job market?
6. What are your major professional accomplishments? What competencies are your strongest calling cards?
7. What are your most notable failures? What did you learn from each?
8. What would your last boss say about your work ethic? What would your coworkers say about you? Your subordinates?
9. What specific things do you require in the job you're seeking – adventure, glamour, a bigger office, more money?

Your Strengths, Abilities, and Values

From the list below circle the words that you believe describe you, and keep them in mind throughout your process:

Active	Goal oriented	Loves animals
Active in sports	Good delegating skills	Loves children
Active reader	Good leadership skills	Loyal
Active volunteer	Good listening skills	Makes friends easily
Adaptable	Good mathematical skills	Moral
Adventurous	Good negotiating skills	Musical
Ambitious	Good presentation skills	Neat
Artistic	Good public speaking skills	Obsessive
Attractive	Good sense of humor	Organized
Brave/heroic	Good team building skills	Passionate
Calm	Good time management skills	Passive
Communicative	Good under pressure	Patient
Computer literate	Good written communicator	Perfectionist

Confident	Graceful	Performer
Courteous	Handles stress well	Physically strong
Creative	Hard-working	Precise
Decisive	High energy	Professional
Dedicated	Highly educated (level)	Quick-thinking
Detail Oriented	Honest	Reacts well to authority
Directed	Introverted	Religious
Dynamic	Learns from mistakes	Responsible
Economical	Left-brained	Right-brained
Efficient	Like people	Risk averse
Empathetic	Likes to travel	Risk taker
Ethical	Logical	Sales personality
Excellent analytical skills		Self-motivated
Excellent math skills		Sports fan
Experienced		Strong-willed
Extroverted		Supportive of others
Flexible		Tenacious
Fluent in other languages		Welcomes change
Focused		Well-groomed

Notes

The 8 Main Question Types

Now we're going to get into the meat of the course. We're going to cover several different question types that you will most likely get during their interview process.

We have covered a total of eight main question types in this book. I believe if you master the art of these eight questions and answer them well, you will have a strong upper hand in any interview.

Don't get me wrong. I'm not claiming that this will comprehensively cover every interview question type out there. But yes, if you master these eight question types your conversations with your interviewers will go very well; in fact, very, very well. Then add on top of that a few technical questions from your field and some administrative questions with HR, and you've gotten yourself close to a 100% chance to get an offer.

Here is how the format of each question type will go:

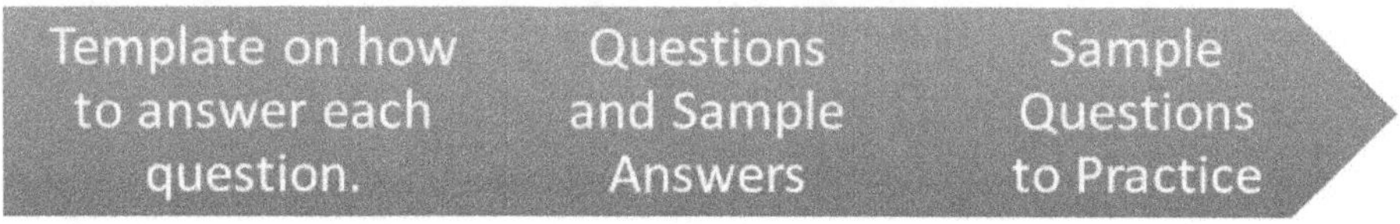

Template on how to answer each question. → Questions and Sample Answers → Sample Questions to Practice

Figure 16 – Approach to Main Question Types

We'll start with a template on how to answer each question type. Then we'll look at a few sample questions and answers. Then I'll give you some homework for you to practice.

Warning

Please do not move forward with any question type till you practice a few questions and start getting confident.

As a reminder, doing your homework is vital as part of the entire process.

Tips When Answering Questions

Here are some general tips to keep in mind when answering questions.

1. Ask clarifying questions before you start.
2. Be decisive.
3. Have conviction.
4. Say a question asks, "Why should we hire you?".
5. Start by saying "I'd love to give you 3 reasons why you should hire me. 1…2…3…". Use this rule of 3 to your advantage.

Explain your reasoning for everything asked.

Framework to Ask Questions – 5W and 1H

A good framework to use when asking questions after an interviewer asks you a question is the following:

5W – Who, When, Why, What, Where

1H – How

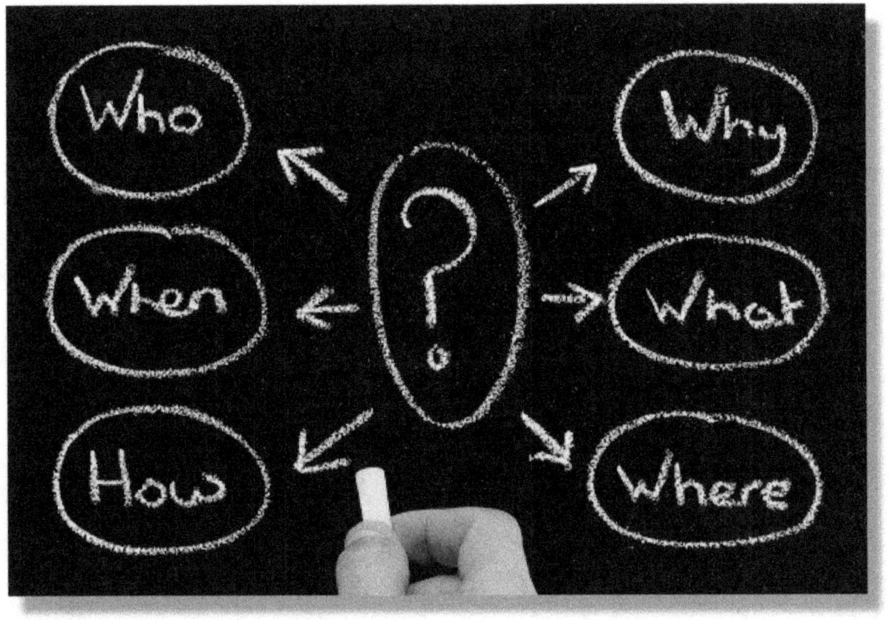

Figure 17 – 5W and 1H Framework to Asking Questions

Use this framework for information gathering during your interview.

The 8 Main Question Types

Now let's now look at the different types of questions.

"Tell me about yourself" Questions

The famous words from almost any interviewer when starting an interview:

Why don't we start by you telling me a little about yourself?

This is probably the first question you will get in any interview that you have, whether it's a recruiter, hiring manager or someone else. So, it is vital that you answer this well. These first few minutes of the conversation is going to set the tone and pace of the rest of the interview.

Your Story

This question is one of the best questions for you to be able to "Tell your Story".

... and that's exactly what it should be.

The answer to this question is not to repeat your resume, but to really showcase your strengths, motivation and fit for the company and job.

Lets see next a framework to answer this question.

Framework to Answer – With Work Experience

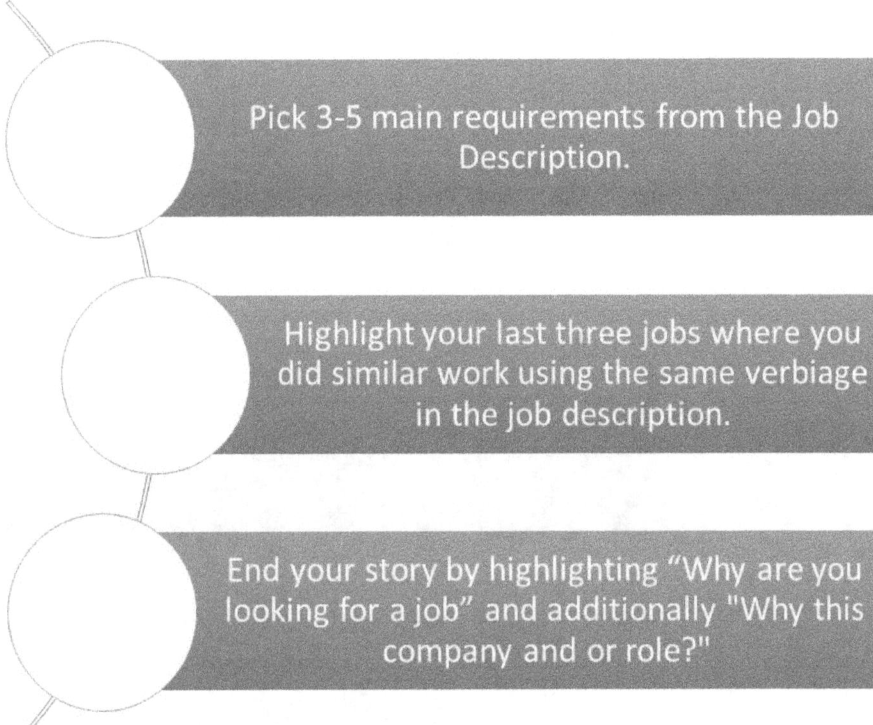

Figure 18 – Your Story (with work experience)

For Each Job – Use This Framework

1. I'm currently <Role A> for <Company B>.
2. As part of this role, I do <Work C> (Using verbiage from the job description).
3. I'd love to highlight <Results D>.
4. Repeat 2-3 times
5. Prior to that I was <Role E> for <Company F>.
6. As part of this role, I did <Work G> (Using verbiage from the job description).
7. I'd love to highlight <Results H>.
8. Additionally, I have <Education I>.
9. I'm leaving my current role because of <Reason J>.
10. And I'm excited about this opportunity with Amazon for the following reasons:

a. <Reason K>
b. <Reason L>
c. Reason M>

Framework to Answer – With NO Work Experience

Pick 3-5 main requirements from the Job Description.

Highlight three projects where you did similar work using the same verbiage in the job description.

End your story by highlighting additionally "Why this company/job?"

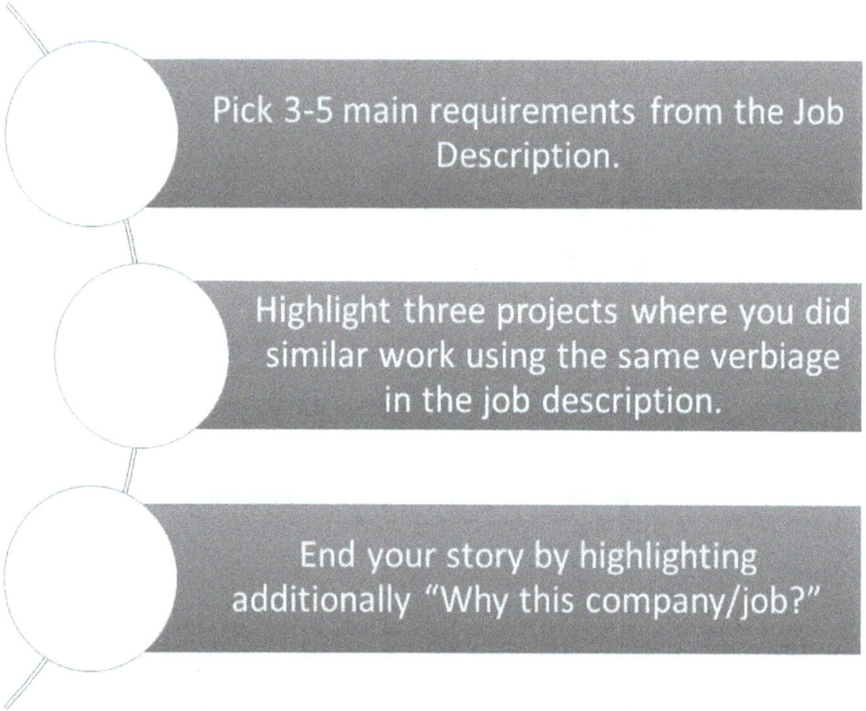

Figure 19 – Your Story (with no work experience)

For Each Project – Use This Framework

1. I'm currently student at <University A> majoring in <Degree B>.
2. As part of studies, I have done <Project C> (Using verbiage from the job description).
3. I'd love to highlight <Results D>.

4. Repeat 2-3 times
5. Additionally, I have done <Project E>.
6. I'd love to highlight <Results F>.
7. I'm excited about this opportunity with the target company for the following reasons:
    a. <Reason K>
    b. <Reason L>
    c. <Reason M>

If we must summarize the story telling process, it involves these 3 steps:

1. This is my background

2. This is why I'm looking

3. This is why I will be a good fit for the role/company

Figure 20 – Framework Around Your Story

Example "Tell me About Yourself" answer

"I'm currently the Chief Operating Officer of Unikrn, an eSports and Gaming technology company based in Seattle, WA. As part of my role, my core responsibility is to work with the management team on the overall strategic plan for Unikrn, including specific goals for the company. But more importantly, drive the individual teams across the company to achieve Unikrn's objectives. My most notable achievement as part of this job to was to take the company from five employees to 40 and to a $7MM Series A round. I believe I've put the company onto a growth path for massive scale in the future.

Prior to that I was a Senior Manager of Product and Strategy at Groupon, where I led an autonomous product and engineering team to launch Groupon's consumer commerce marketplace on its web platform. This project added 2MM active users to Groupon's web platform in Q3 of 2015, a growth of 25% from the previous quarter.

Additionally, I've spent six years at Microsoft as an Engineering Manager leading teams between five and 40 in the Office, Windows, and Dynamics groups. My most notable achievement was the launch of the online app store for Windows 8. This enabled Microsoft for the first time to compete effectively with Apple by creating its own app platform.

Also, I have a Masters in Computer Science from Clemson University and an MBA from The University of Chicago, Booth School of Business in Entrepreneurship, Finance, and Strategy.

I've started exploring opportunities recently due to significant change in the direction of my company. The co-founders have decided to move the company to Australia, something that I can't do personally at this point of time. Hence, I'm very excited to interview with your firm.

I normally look for 3 criteria when looking for new companies:

Companies that offer products and services that solve a true need for its customers.

A role that gives me an opportunity to drive product and engineering teams to achieve company goals.

A culture that encourages entrepreneurship and an action oriented attitude.

Amazon and this role specifically has hit the checkboxes for these criteria and I firmly believe we'll both be a great fit to each other."

Tips

Don't focus on the negatives of any previous job experience. Make sure to spin any negative into a positive.

For example:

- Never complain about your current role.
- Never focus on money.
- Never focus on being bored and not learning.

Homework

It's your turn now.

Please practice this question multiple times as it will be your "ice breaker" question in any interview.

Plus, it will showcase your confidence and communication skills as you kick things off in an interview.

Here are some questions to ponder over:

1. Tell me about yourself.
2. Tell me a little more about what you've been doing over the past few years.
3. What brings you here to this opportunity?
4. Why are you leaving your current job?

"Why" Questions?

These are questions that ask you questions around "Why this job?", "Why this role?" Etc. Etc.

Anything that starts with a "Why"?

These questions will most definitely be asked by the recruiter in your first phone screen and by the hiring manager when you speak to him or her.

These are great ways to understand your motivation and just like the 'Tell me about yourself" questions, these are great ice breakers and ways to start conversations off.

Framework to Answer

Use the Rule of 3

Probably one of the oldest rules in the book – The Rule of 3. Give exactly 3 points when answering these questions.

Next let's look at a framework to specifically answer these question types.

Framework to Answer – Why Company?

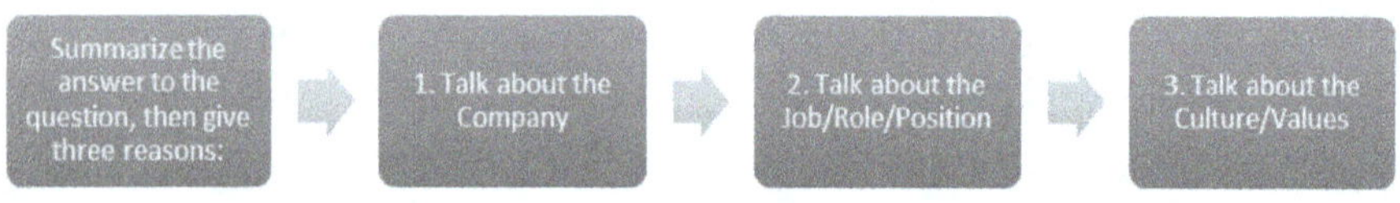

Figure 21 – "Why Company?" Framework

Again, a reminder of why I asked you before to study the company, its culture, values etc.

Framework to Answer – Why Role?

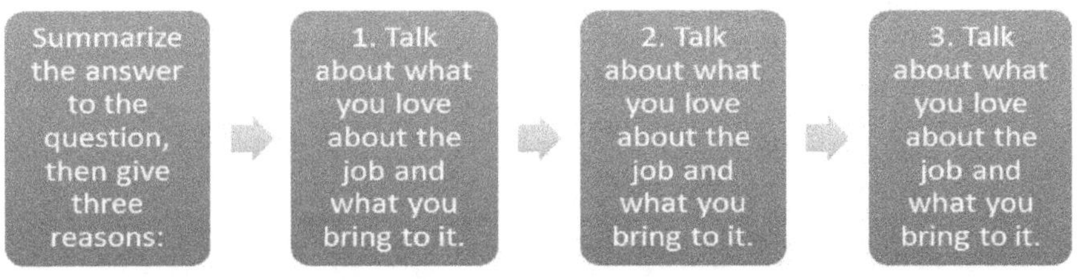

Figure 22 – "Why Role?" Framework

Framework to Answer – Why Industry?

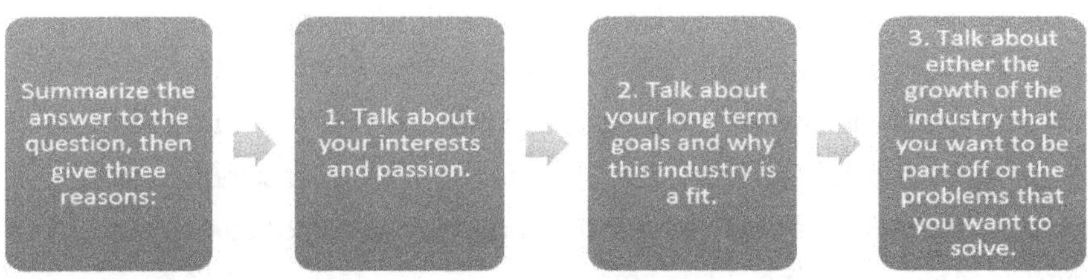

Figure 23 – "Why Company?" Framework

3 Typical Examples

The next three examples are typical examples that we've seen in and out in almost every interview we've been part off.

So, we highly recommend practicing these two examples before you go into your interview.

We have also provided model answers that you can use to help you prepare for your [Job Title] role.

"Why Company?"

"Why Position"?

"Why Industry"?

Example – Why Company?

Question: Why do you want to join us at Amazon?

"There are 3 main reasons why I'd like to join Amazon:

Amazon over the past few years has been on a strong path of innovation, specifically in the cloud space. The company has come up with interesting services on the cloud such as Kindle Direct Publishing and Fulfillment by Amazon that have taken the world by storm. I want to work for an innovative company that is poised to change the world through its innovative products and services. I strongly believe that winning companies are those that constantly innovate and are ahead of the market. Amazon is one such company.

Secondly, I'm excited about what I bring to the company. My experience and passion has been in supporting products and services and I have done that over my 10-year career in my previous roles. I'm excited about bringing this experience and passion to Amazon and help successfully support many innovate products affecting millions of customers.

Thirdly, culture is very important to me. I thrive well in entrepreneurial cultures. The Amazon principles of leadership "Taking Ownership" and "Taking Action" appeal to my style of operating on a day to day basis and I believe I'll be able to perform at my peak there."

Example – Why Role?

Question: Why do you want to be a Customer Support Representative (CSR)?

"There are 3 specific reasons why the role of a CSR is appealing to me:

CSRs are representatives of the customer. *I believe that the most successful businesses focus their attention on the customer. I also believe that CSRs represent the customer. It's through this role of representing the customer that I cannot make only make an impact to our customers, but also help communicate their needs and wants internally. Through this role, I can directly influence customers and hence the business.*

Good CSRs can sell *– Additionally, I do believe some of the best CSRs can also cross sell or cross promote other products on the company. This is another skill of mine. I believe by focusing on the customer and using my ability to sell, I help customers get what they want, but at the same time grow the company's business.*

Finally, CSRs communicate cross functionally *– My personal leadership style is all about leading via influence, irrespective of whether I have reports or not. Great CSRs are relationship builders specifically with the internal product teams as they communicate requirements back from the customer. The ability to communicate cross functionally is one of my key strengths that makes me a good fit to this role."*

Example – Why Industry?

Question: Why are you interested in joining the tech sector?

"There are 3 main reasons why I'd love to join the technology industry:

My Personal Interests and Passion – As I was going through my undergraduate year in college, I started meeting with a few alumni Customer Support Managers at Amazon from my university and started developing a keen interest for the CSR role, specifically in the tech sector. I loved the challenge of owning a technology product and working with customers to get that product operational for them.

Secondly, my long-term goals play an important part in my decision. In the long run, I see myself starting my own technology company. I believe the best CEOs are very customer driven. They can think strategically about the market dynamics, but more importantly, can deliver a value proposition towards the needs and wants of the customer.

Finally, the tech industry is at the forefront of innovation in every industry. Technology is working today on problems for the future. That's what excites me about this industry.

So, it's this combination of my personal passion, my long-term goals and the opportunity that this industry brings that attracts me to this industry."

Homework

This is the list of questions you should be ready for in your interview:

1. Why this company?
2. Why do you want to work here?
3. Why this job/role?
4. Why not go to <Company X>?
5. Why the <Industry> industry?
6. I don't think the <Industry> industry is for you. Explain.

"Goals" Questions

This is the next set of questions that you should prepare for. There are two questions here that you should be ready with.

1. What are your short-term goals?
2. What are your long-term goals?

Framework to Answer – Long Term Goals

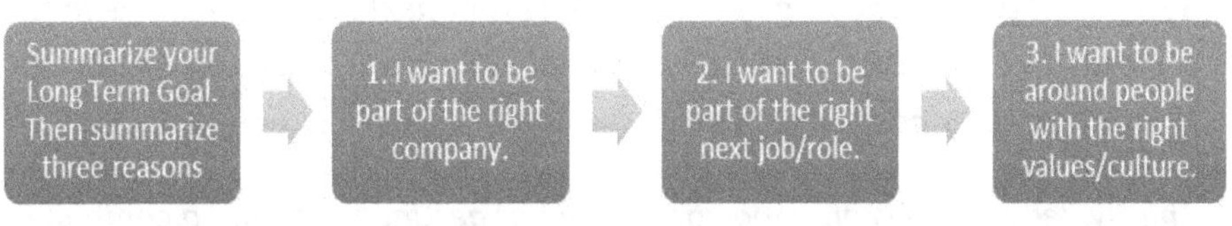

Figure 24 – Long Term Goals Framework

Framework to Answer – Short Term Goals

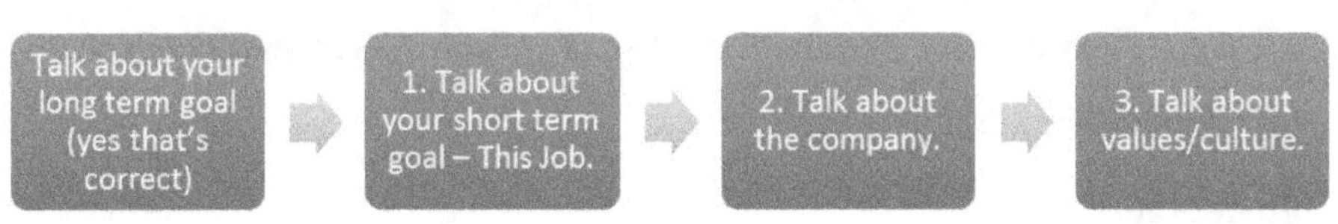

Figure 25 – Short Term Goals Framework

Example – What are your long-term goals?

"In the long run, i.e. over the next 10 years, I see myself becoming the

General Manager of a Business Unit at Amazon, where I can run various cross functional teams and manage P&L to be able to successfully execute on company goals.

To get there:

I want to work for a company that encourages my long-term plan and provides a growth part for me.

Secondly, I believe the role of a CSR is the great next step for me. I believe the best CEOs are customer focused people who can think critically about customers, their needs and wants.

Thirdly, leadership is an important aspect of getting there and a company such as Amazon and its leadership principles put me a strong growth path to getting there."

Example – What are your short-term goals?

"I'd like to start by outlining my long-term goal. I see myself becoming the General Manager of a Business Unit at Amazon, where I can run various cross functional teams and manage P&L to be able to successfully execute on company goals.

To get there:

My short-term goal is find a position that puts me on the path towards the long run. In my case, the CSR. I aspire to grow in that role, prove myself and then to expand that out to becoming a Customer Support Manager managing a team of people to support our customers.

Additionally, I'd want to do this at a company such as Amazon that encourages growth this kind of growth.

Thirdly, leadership is an important aspect of getting there and a company such as Amazon and its leadership principles put me a strong growth path to getting there."

"Strengths and Weaknesses" Questions

The next type of question is the **"Strengths and Weaknesses"** questions.

Another extremely important type of question that is going to be asked to you through the entire process.

So, it's best to be well prepared.

Like before, the goal here is to use the "Rule of 3". Give exactly three strengths and three weaknesses.

Additionally, for your weaknesses you will need to also add the following: "What have you been doing to overcome your weakness".

Let's look at details...

Strengths – Framework to Answer

Focus on the core strengths of your position – the ones we discussed in step 4, when we looked at the job description. You want to be able to highlight those skills.

Bonus points if you highlight 3 strengths that has verbiage directly from the job description. Let's look at a framework to answer this question.

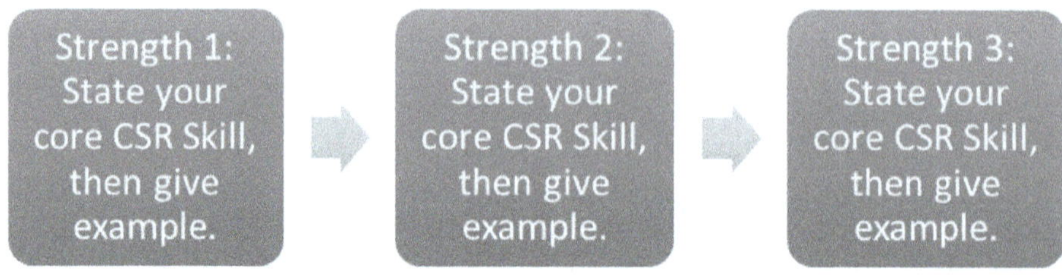

Figure 26 – Strengths Framework

Example "Give me Your Top Strengths"

"Absolutely. I believe I have three top strengths that I'd like to highlight and they are as follows:

I'm extremely analytical. *As an example, this one time using insights on our customers, I was able to significantly influence a change in our overall customer support strategy. I noticed in our data that there were not a lot of repeat purchases by our customers. This insight that I put forward to my team helped us change our strategy where we started selling our products to customers. I make tons of my decisions based on the data which enables me to keep any biases out of the equation.*

I believe I have strong leadership skills. *The ability to influence others and bring the best out from them is a core strength of mine. I didn't have any direct reports in my last job, but was successfully able to pitch the idea around better customer support operations to my manager.*

Finally, ***I'm relentless and see things through.*** *In my first job as a CSR at Microsoft, there were tons of bugs in one of our older products that management had given up on due to the volume of bugs. This was an opportunity for me to step in, prioritize those bugs and communicate it back to the product managers working on the project. When we launched, the project earned tons of kudos for both me and our department in general and was considered a huge success for the company."*

Weaknesses – Framework to Answer

Be honest here and don't give something vague like "I work too hard".

Pick a genuine weakness.

Be professional and talk about work related weaknesses, as compared to something personal.

Finally, make sure you mention what you are doing to overcome this weakness.

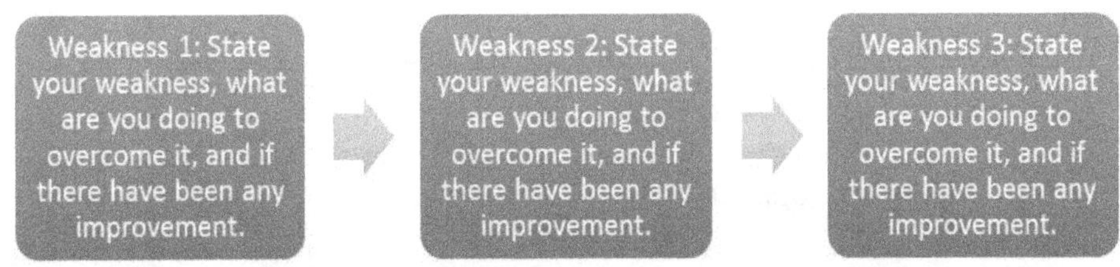

Figure 27 – Weaknesses Framework

Example – What's Your Biggest Weakness?

"In my last performance review, my boss wrote that "John has a straightforward and direct approach. For those not familiar with John, they will be taken aback by John's bluntness and find it offensive."

The reason I am blunt is that I get impatient with others. I am eager for my team to do a job and do it well. Over the last 3 years, I've worked on becoming more patient by:

Meditating. It helps be calmer and contemplative.

Be more compassionate. I have begun to accept that not everyone can operate by my standards.

Take time for breaks. Whether it's exercise or grabbing a beer with co-workers, it helps me break me away from the must-get-it-done routine.

Recently, my peers & direct reports have noticed a change in my behavior. One person told me, "John you're more laid back now. Small things don't seem to bother you as much. You've been more patient with others, and your working relationships have improved."

Strengths and Weaknesses

Sometimes employers will ask you questions related to both your Strengths and Weaknesses. The key is to answer both.

For example: You could be asked – "What would your coworkers have to say about you?".

The key to this question is to recognize that the interviewer is trying to see whether you are critical about yourself, but at the same time you recognize your strengths.

Sample Strengths

Here is a list of strengths that you can key off for your interview.

analytical	scrappy	creative
energetic	organized	decisive
Thinking outside the box	Risk taking	Calm under pressure
thorough	See things through	Understand people's feelings
flexible	initiative	Detail-oriented
Good planner	quantitative	multitasking
leadership	Good to taking feedback	persistent
persuasive	Data-driven	independent
Self-critical	Good mentor; caring	Not afraid of challenges
prioritization	Enjoy learning new skills	Add humor and fun to the team

Figure 28 – Sample Strengths

Sample Weaknesses

Similarly, here is a list of weaknesses.

Not detail oriented	Overly confident	Lack of confidence
Too negative	Makes too many assumptions	unrealistic
unassertive	impatient	indecisive
stubborn	Intimidating to others	procrastinator
Take feedback personally	Difficulty admitting failure	Hesitant asking for help
Too direct/blunt	overanalyzing	argumentative
Easily distracted	Can be very vague	Bad at multitasking
Micromanages people	Short attention span	shy

Figure 29 – Sample Weaknesses

Homework

Strengths

1. What are some of your strong points?
2. Tell me your strengths.
3. What would be reasons we would promote you at your job?
4. Why should we hire you?
5. What's your style of leadership?

Weaknesses

1. What are some of your weaknesses?
2. If you are not here in this company one year from now, what do you think would be the reasons?

Strengths and Weaknesses

1. If I ask your ex-boss/coworker about you, what would they say?

"Tell me about a time" Questions

Example: "Tell me about a time when you successfully shipped a feature".

This is probably the most important set of questions that you will get.

Companies have started asking tons of these and they will NOT stop after your first answer. They will consistently dig deeper looking for deeper answers to the answer to ensure that you are a good fit.

Before we get into the heart of the types of questions and how to prepare for this, let's look at a framework to answer this question type.

Framework to Answer

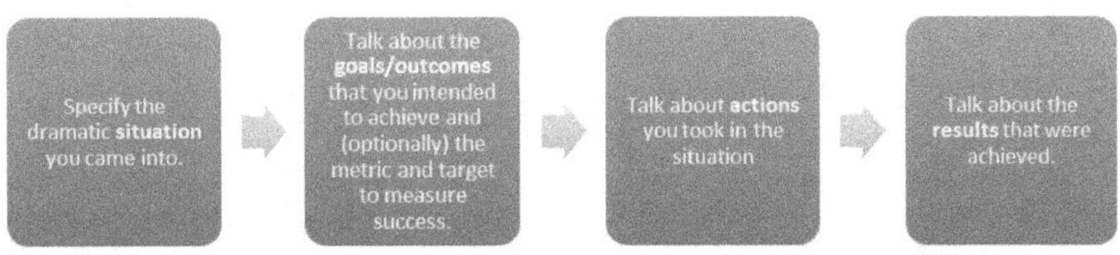

Figure 30 – SGAR Framework

This is what we like to call the SGAR framework.

Situation, Goals, Actions, Results (SGAR)

5 Main Categories

Normally these questions fall into the following five categories: Leadership and Influence, Challenges, Mistakes/Failures, Successes, and Teamwork.

Category	Example
Leadership and Influence	Tell me about a time when you made a decision that wasn't popular.
Challenges	Tell me about a time when you weren't able to reach a deadline.
Mistakes/Failures	Tell me about a time when you failed.
Successes	Tell me about a time when you solved a problem in a creative way.
Teamwork	Tell me about a time when you had to do something you didn't want to do.

Figure 31 – 5 Main Categories to Practice

What do the Categories Mean?

Leadership and Influence – is all about influencing other people to bring the best work out of them with or without direct responsibility over them, so an interviewer will want to understand what tactics you use to build teams, persuade, or influence others.

Challenges – The interviewer is looking not just for challenges that you faced in your job or in your personal life, but how did you deal with them. The interviewer is looking for how you solve problems.

Mistakes and Failures – For one the interviewer is looking for your humbleness in admitting that you failed or made a mistake. Secondly, she or he is looking for how you handled the situation appropriately.

When Talking About Mistakes

- Please avoid anything that will represent a red flag to the company.

- Don't go overboard.

For example: Giving an example of when you lied or cheated is going NOT going to help here.

Successes – This is another opportunity to sell yourself. Use this opportunity to talk about a project in your past where you made the most impact, but at the same time its relevancy for the role.

Teamwork – Teamwork questions are used to assess your interpersonal skills, particularly in times when you are working with your immediate peers. Communication, especially in areas of diverse cultural and "working style" settings will be useful to highlight.

Example – Leadership and Influence

Question: Tell me about a time when you were leading a team that faced a significant challenge, and how you led your team to overcome that challenge.

"We had a final class project during business school where we needed to deconstruct a business case scenario and make a formal presentation. I was elected team leader to make sure things stayed on track and to take the lead in the presentation. Everyone got along fine at first – we were making good progress on understanding the key issues the business faced – but as we neared the deadline, we couldn't agree on what the solutions were for those key issues. People simply disagreed, and given that everyone was tired and stressed, it led to a lot of fighting and tempers really flared.

The problem was that the team had essentially two opposing views of the solution. I tried to wait it out a bit, but it seemed like we were getting nowhere, so eventually I took the lead and simply said, "Look, you guys appointed me as your team lead, so this is what I propose." Then, I laid out a compromise solution that had parts of each side's thoughts. Next, I pointedly asked each person, one at a time, if they were okay with this solution, and if they weren't, what their concerns were. By doing this, I really isolated the problems and made sure to get buy-in.

Miraculously, we could finish the project on time and we got a great grade. What I took from this experience was two-fold: one, that as a leader your job is to make sure the team delivers on key deadlines and deliverables, and two, that both individual and group buy-in are necessary to move forward and reduce friction."

Example – Challenges

Question: How did you deal with a difficult boss?

"My manager in my last job, where I worked for two years, was tough. Really tough. I struggled the first few months I worked with him – in retrospect, I realized that I had no idea what he wanted from me.

So finally, I decided I couldn't take it anymore, so I scheduled a lunch with him to address the issue. At lunch, I basically said that I was having a challenging time working under him. Then I gave him three examples of where I'd spent an enormous amount of time working on a specific assignment, only to have him change what he wanted at the last minute. I then talked about how I could've done five other things for him and helped the company if I hadn't wasted that time.

He was a little taken aback, but because I was so specific about the opportunities to use time that would have been freed up had he been more direct and consistent, he really took to it. After that, I think he respected me a whole lot more. He really listened, and became more thoughtful about his early decisions so he didn't change directions 180 degrees at the last minute. I took away from that experience the need to be facts-based when having sensitive conversations, and to show how resolving a conflict can benefit both parties by really trying to see priorities and concerns from someone else's perspective."

Example – Mistakes/Failures

Question: What was your greatest failure and what lessons did you learn from it?

"I tried to start an organization on campus my freshman year, but in the end, it failed. The main goal of the organization was to help new students from China coming in to the United States settle in well.

It was far from a waste of time, however – I learned so much about what it takes to start something and keep it going. I realized that I didn't plan thoroughly enough and that I tried to go too fast.

With that experience under my belt, I successfully started a consulting club on campus my junior year to get together with like-minded students regularly to study cases and talk about business trends. My team and I grew the club to 300 members in the first year through effective advertising. We have a great funding model, and we continue to go above and beyond the mission we set out to accomplish."

Example – Successes

Question: What do you think is your biggest success?

"My biggest success professionally has been taking my company from Pre-Revenue to $5MM a year over a period of two years.

When I started the company, unlike many startups, I decided to put together a clear-cut business plan and associated with that a strategic plan on how I was going to get there over the period of two years. I broke down the bigger plan into smaller pieces and set quarterly and monthly goals. Then I started executing on the plan, consistently built my team over time and one step at a time achieved the goals I initially set out.

This experience taught me the power of planning and discipline when it came to achieving goals. My consistent discipline is the big reason that I was able to achieve my company goals"

Example – Teamwork

Question: How would you deal with difficult coworkers?

"I was a writer for the sports coverage desk of the campus newspaper. There were just four of us, including one section leader, and we spent all of our time together going to events – watching them, discussing them, and then writing our stories. There was one guy who was just tough to be around. Every time I proposed a story, he tossed out a sarcastic comment in response. And he always pointed out little things about my story that were vague or wordy. It was hard to work with him. I noticed that over time due to this behavior we were unable to hit some of our deadlines.

I finally sat down with him one day when everyone else had left the office. I was really direct with him about how what he was doing affected me. He was defensive, but then I started to give examples of his bothersome behavior.

I also showed him that I appreciated his eye for detail, but shared how constructive criticism would sound to me (it was different to his approach, that's for sure!) I think what really got across was my general message of, 'Look, we both want to write great articles and give people good recaps of games and stories about the teams. I'm happy if you criticize my writing to help me make it better, but in the future, why don't we sit together and try to help improve each other's stuff as opposed to trying to embarrass the other person in front of a group?'

I learned a lot – specifically that sometimes things can get personal, but I needn't react defensively. Rather than focusing on feelings, I need to show where goals overlap and propose actual steps we can take to fix the problem together. Overtime, our relationship improved and I started receiving more constructive feedback on my writing. Over the next couple of months, we started receiving praise for our writings and we hadn't missed a single deadline"

How to Prepare? Prepare 15 Main Stories and Spin Them

For each of the five categories we discussed above, prepare three stories using our framework and list them down using the "Stories" worksheet provided.

Category	Job 1	Job 2	Personal
Leadership and Influence			
Teamwork			
Successes			
Challenges			
Mistakes/Failures			

Figure 32 – Stories Worksheet

Job Description and Stories

Remember I asked you to study the job description. Now is the time to showcase those in your interview.

This is your time to highlight those here in your cheat sheet. You must lead with those in your interview.

That way you're consistently focusing on the language of the company.

Final Cheat Sheet for Stories

So, your final cheat sheet would look something like this, with the important ones highlighted.

Category	Job 1	Job 2	Personal
Leadership and Influence			
Teamwork			
Successes			
Challenges			
Mistakes/Failures			
	Additional Story from the highlights in the job description		
		Additional Story from the highlights in the job description	

Figure 33 – Final Stories Worksheet

Homework – Leadership and Influence

1. Describe a decision you made that wasn't popular. How did you handle implementing it?
2. Describe a time when you had to motivate employees as coworkers.

3. Tell me about a time when you showed initiative.
4. Tell me about a time when you had to give a presentation to people who disagreed with you.
5. Tell me about a time when you had to make an unpopular decision.
6. Tell me about a time when you had to sell another person or team on your idea.
7. Tell me about a time when you've built a team.

Homework – Challenges

1. Tell me about a time when you faced a challenge and overcame it.
2. Tell me about a time when you couldn't reach a deadline.
3. Describe a major change that occurred in a job that you held. How did you adapt to this change?
4. Tell me about a time when you had to deal with changing priorities. How did you handle it?
5. Tell me about a time when you had to decide quickly or with insufficient data.
6. Tell me about a time when you used a lot of data in a short period of time.
7. Tell me about a time when you handled a risky situation.

Homework – Mistakes and Failures

1. Tell me about a time when you made a mistake.
2. Tell me about a time when you failed.
3. Tell me about a time you improperly analyzed a situation.
4. Tell me about a time when you were disappointed with yourself.

5. Tell me about a time when you were unable to judge all your responsibilities.

Homework – Success

1. Tell me about something you're proud of accomplishing.
2. Tell me about a time when you reached a goal that was important.
3. Tell me about a specific insight you gained from something outside of work.
4. Tell me about a time when you went above and beyond the call of duty.
5. Describe a time when you resolved a situation before it became serious.
6. Tell me about a time when you had to show innovation.
7. Tell me about a time when you solved a problem in a creative way.

Homework – Teamwork

1. Tell me about a time when you had to work across teams to accomplish something.
2. Tell me about a time when you had a disagreement at work.
3. Tell me about a time when you mentored or aided a coworker.
4. Tell me about a time when you had to do something you didn't want to do.
5. Tell me about a time when you had to compromise.
6. Tell me about a time when you had to resolve a conflict.
7. Tell me about a time when you had a challenging interaction with a coworker.

"Cultural and Values" Questions

Remember our "Strengths, Motivation and Fit" framework initially. This type of question focuses on your fit to the company.

The hiring team wants to know whether they can tolerate working with you and if you'll be a good fit to the team, their values and how they operate every day.

Most of these should already be covered in the previous section, however, make sure that there are aspects of the culture that you are not missing.

Example – What do you like to do for fun?

"In my free time, I love to read books. I'm currently reading a book called "Play Bigger.

The book discusses how some of the fastest growing companies are category creators. They taught customers a new way of doing things. The book outlines something known as "Category Creation Strategy" by learning and summarizing from the best category creators of this world – the likes of Facebook, Uber among others."

How to Prepare?

Remember our "Company" worksheet, where I asked you list out everything related to the company – specifically its culture and values. Now it's time to bring all that together.

Pick areas of the culture/values section from that sheet and practice one example for each.

You don't need to use the entire SGAR framework. Simply state your answer and justify why.

4. Culture:

5. Values:

Figure 34 – Culture and Values from Company Worksheet

Prepare one example from each cultural area and one from values.

Category	Example
Culture Area 1	
Culture Area 2	
Values 1	
Values 2	
...	

Figure 35 – Culture and Values Examples

Homework

1. What books do you read?
2. What do you like to do outside work?
3. What do you do for fun?
4. What are some of your hobbies?
5. Tell me a joke.

"Resume" Questions

These questions specifically pin point an area on your resume and ask you to detail more about it. This is nothing but a variation of our "Tell me about a time" set of questions. The main difference being that they focus specifically on an area that you've listed.

Framework to Answer

Don't worry – you already got this. SGAR (Situation, Goals, Action, Results)

Homework

1. I see you've listed project X on your resume. Can you describe the experience in more detail?

"What Would You Do" Questions

These questions are very specific to the role that you are interviewing for.

For example: If you are interviewing for a customer service position, the question could be:

What would you do if an angry customer walks in the door and starts yelling?

For example: If you are interviewing for a sales associate position, the question could be:

What if you had to sell a pen to someone, how would you do it?

"Tell me about a time" was real. "What would you do" is about the hypothetical.

In short, this is putting you in a hypothetical situation and the interviewer wants to see how you'd react.

Framework to Answer

1. Start by asking questions to get a thorough understanding of the question. Please look at our 5W and 1H framework to ask questions.
2. Take notes throughout. Use either a notepad or a whiteboard.
3. In your mind, start thinking of the framework you will be applying. Think in your head, if this was a theoretical question, what framework would you use to answer this question. DO NOT GIVE THE FRAMEWORK OUT TO YOUR INTERVIEWER.
4. Start applying the framework to the situation in hand, improvise as necessary. GIVE SPECIFICS.

Summarize your points and make a conclusion.

Homework

1. Go to glassdoor.com and find out the top 10 most common questions in the category/company you are interviewing for. Specifically, you should be looking at these "case based" or "hypothetical" or "what would you do" type of questions.
2. Write down the general framework that you would use for those 10 questions.
3. Then practice each question using the approach shown here, applying the framework to each question from glass door.

BONUS – "Money" Questions

Money questions are common throughout the process of interviewing. So, it's important to have an answer ready. For example: You will be asked the question "What are you currently making and what would you like to make in the future?".

Most candidates give their current salary which boxes their future package. Others don't give a number at all, which risks getting a low offer.

Instead I would like to present to you an alternate framework to answer this question.

At the end of the day, what you truly desire is to get paid what you are worth. So, a better framework to answer would be:

1. Give a wide range. I really mean a wide range. For example: *"Over the past few years, I've been making between $50,000 and $200,000."*
2. State that you are open and would love the opportunity to work for the company and that if you get to the state where money is discussed say that you would be open to working something out.
3. State your value and why money shouldn't matter to the company if you are able to create more value.
4. NEVER GIVE A NUMBER.

An example answer would be something as follows:

"Over the past five years or so, I've been making between $50,000 and $200,000, so I'm open. If we get to the stage that we start discussing money, we can certainly pin down a number that works for both of us.

At the end of the day, I want to make sure that I give you enough value that money shouldn't be the concern for you as I'll be able to make my salary and much more back to the company.

I'm excited about the opportunity and would love to take the conversation forward."

Stories Cheat Sheet

Category	Job 1	Job 2	Personal
Leadership and Influence			
Teamwork			
Successes			

Challenges			
Mistakes and Failures			

Category	Job 1	Job 2	Personal
Additional Job Responsibility from Job Description ________________			
Additional Job Responsibility from Job Description ________________			
Additional Job Responsibility from Job Description ________________			

Additional Job Responsibility from Job Description ____________________			
Additional Job Responsibility from Job Description ____________________			
Additional Job Responsibility from Job Description ____________________			

Culture/Value	Example
Culture ______________________	
Culture ______________________	
Culture ______________________	
Culture ______________________	

Value ______________________________	
Value ______________________________	
Value ______________________________	
Value ______________________________	

Main Question Types Homework Summary

Tell me about yourself

1. Tell me about yourself.
2. Tell me a little more about what you've been doing over the past few years.
3. What brings you here to this opportunity?
4. Why are you leaving your current job?

Why

1. Why this company?
2. Why do you want to work here?
3. Why this job/role?
4. Why not go to <Company X>?
5. Why <Industry X>?
6. I don't think <Industry X> is for you.

Goals

1. What are your short-term goals?
2. What are your long-term goals?

Strengths and Weaknesses

3. **Strengths**

1. What are some of your strong points?
2. Tell me your strengths.
3. What would be reasons we would promote you at your job?
4. Why should we hire you?

4. **Weaknesses**

1. What are some of your weaknesses?
2. If you are not here in this company one year from now, what do you think would be the reasons?

5. **Strengths and Weaknesses**

1. If I ask your ex-boss/coworker about you, what would they say?

Tell me about a time

Leadership and Influence

1. Describe a decision you made that wasn't popular. How did you handle implementing it?
2. Describe a time when you had to motivate employees as coworkers.
3. Tell me about a time when you showed initiative.
4. Tell me about a time when you showed initiative.

5. Tell me about a time when you had to give a presentation to people who disagreed with you.
6. Tell me about a time when you had to make an unpopular decision.
7. Tell me about a time when you had to sell another person or team on your idea.
8. Tell me about a time when you've built a team.

Challenges

1. Tell me about a time when you faced a challenge and overcame it.
2. Tell me about a time when you couldn't reach a deadline.
3. Describe a major change that occurred in a job that you held. How did you adapt to this change?
4. Tell me about a time when you had to deal with changing priorities. How did you handle it?
5. Tell me about a time when you had to decide quickly or with insufficient data.
6. Tell me about a time when you used a lot of data in a short period of time.
7. Tell me about a time when you handled a risky situation.

Mistakes and Failures

1. Tell me about a time when you made a mistake.
2. Tell me about a time when you failed.
3. Tell me about a time you improperly analyzed a situation.
4. Tell me about a time when you were disappointed with yourself.
5. Tell me about a time when you were unable to judge all your responsibilities.

Success

1. Tell me about something you're proud of accomplishing.
2. Tell me about a time when you reached a goal that was important.
3. Tell me about a specific insight you gained from something outside of work.
4. Tell me about a time when you went above and beyond the call of duty.
5. Describe a time when you resolved a situation before it became serious.
6. Tell me about a time when you had to show innovation.
7. Tell me about a time when you solved a problem in a creative way.

Teamwork

1. Tell me about a time when you had to work across teams to accomplish something.
2. Tell me about a time when you had a disagreement at work.
3. Tell me about a time when you mentored or aided a coworker.
4. Tell me about a time when you had to do something you didn't want to do.
5. Tell me about a time when you had to compromise.
6. Tell me about a time when you had to resolve a conflict.
7. Tell me about a time when you had a challenging interaction with a coworker.

Culture

1. What work environment motivates you?
2. When have you been the most successful in your career?
3. How books do you read?
4. What do you like to do outside work?
5. What do you do for fun?
6. What are some of your hobbies?
7. Tell me a joke.

Resume

1. I see you've listed project X on your resume. Can you describe the experience in more detail?

What would you do

From Glassdoor, Top 10 hypothetical questions that are asked many times during an interview in your category/company.

Question 1

____

____

____

____

____

Framework to Answer Question

____

____

____

____

____

____

____

____

Question 2

____

____

____

____

____

Framework to Answer Question

____

____

____

____

____

____

____

____

____

____

____

____

____

____

____

____

Question 3

Framework to Answer Question

Question 4

Framework to Answer Question

Question 5

Framework to Answer Question

Question 6

Framework to Answer Question

Question 7

Framework to Answer Question

Question 8

Framework to Answer Question

Question 9

Framework to Answer Question

Question 10

Framework to Answer Question

Notes

Chapter 9 – Step 6 - Practice, Practice, Practice

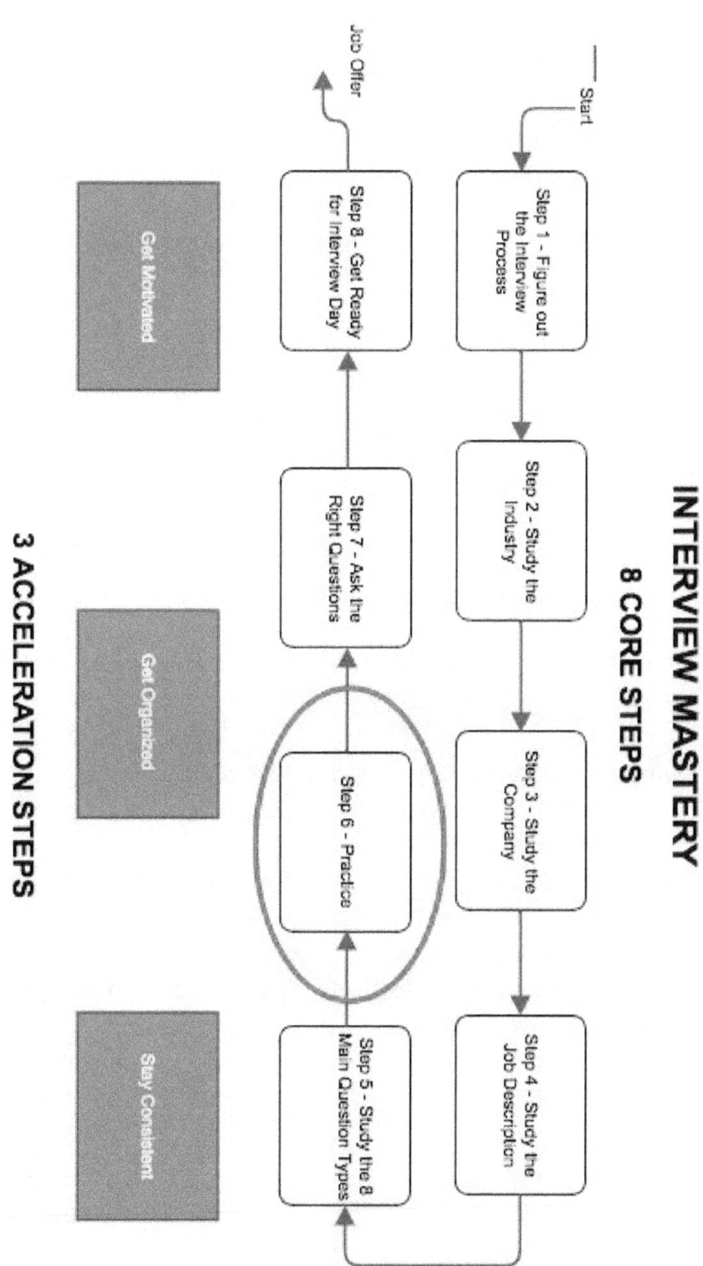

Figure 36 – The 8 x 3 Interview Mastery Framework – Step 6

Now it's time to get down and dirty and practice. You'll have to practice tons and tons of questions before you feel extremely confident for your upcoming interview.

I have a total of 99 questions for practice. Please go through each of them one after the other. Use everything you've learnt so far.

Note that some of these questions are difficult and we will use multiple concepts we've seen so far.

For example: For certain questions, you might need to showcase your "Strengths" and your "Goals".

Homework

What I'd like you to do is to use the "Practice Questions" worksheet (if needed) to practice these 99 questions before your upcoming interview.

For any difficult questions, mark down which concepts would apply to those questions and how you would answer them.

The best way to practice them is to do the following:

1. Look at a question.
2. Answer it loudly. No, not in your head. Answer is loudly as if you're speaking to yourself.
3. Reflect on the question after you're done.
4. Use the "Practice Questions" worksheet to take notes and practice is once more.

Practice Questions Worksheet

Question:

____

____

____

____

Write down thoughts from the appropriate concept to answer this question. Mix and match as necessary.

Strengths, Motivations, and Fit Framework

____

____

____

____

Understanding "You"

____

____

____

____

"Tell me about yourself" questions

____

____

____

____

"Why" questions

____

____

____

____

"Goals" questions

____

____

____

____

"Strengths and Weaknesses" questions

____

____

____

____

"Tell me about a time" questions

____

____

____

____

"Cultural" questions

____

____

____

____

"Resume" questions

____

____

____

____

"What would you do" questions

Bonus: Money questions

List of Practice Questions

Here is a detailed list of top interview questions for you to review. When you come across questions that you "hope you are never asked" – highlight these so you can research and brainstorm on your responses. This will help you to feel confident, prepared, and excited for your interviews!

1. Why do you want to work for us?
2. How do you feel you can help our company/organization?
3. If you were choosing someone for this job, what kind of person would you select?
4. If you could have your choice of any job, what would you do?
5. Why do you want to go into the ______________ field?
6. If you feel you have any weakness with regard to this job, what would it be?
7. What do you expect in this job that you were not getting in your past jobs?
8. What does your spouse think about the kind of work you do? How about this job?
9. How do you feel about evening work?
10. Assuming we make you an offer, what do you see as your future?
11. How would you handle this problem? (After interviewer describes problem)
12. Are you considering other positions at this time? How does this one compare with them?
13. Why did you leave your last job?
14. How long have you been out of work?
15. What have you been doing since you left your last job?
16. How did you like working at ____________company? Why?
17. What are your short range/long range goals? How do you expect to meet them?
18. What does success mean to you? How do you judge it?
19. What are the things that motivate you?

20. Do you plan to get further education, degrees?
21. What have you done to improve yourself during the last year?
22. How do you spend your spare time?
23. Tell me about your health.
24. If you could re live your last 15 years, what changes would you make?
25. Tell me about your greatest achievement / disappointment in life.
26. What are some of your weaknesses?
27. What did you like best/least about your last job?
28. In your last job, how much of the work did you do on your own, and how much as part of a team? Which did you enjoy more?
29. What are some of the more difficult problems you encountered in your past jobs? How did you solve them?
30. Did you ever make any suggestions to management? What happened?
31. What do you think management could do to make you function more effectively as an employee?
32. What has kept you from progressing as fast as you would have liked?
33. Tell me about your family.
34. What does your husband/wife do?
35. What else do you think I should know about you?
36. Tell me about the best/worst boss you ever had.
37. Everybody likes to criticize. What do people criticize about you?
38. Everybody has pet peeves. What are yours?
39. What is your leadership style?
40. Are you geographically mobile, either now, or in the future?
41. Isn't this a career switch?
42. Do you think your education qualifies you for this position? (When applicant does not have a degree.)
43. You don't have the experience/background for this position. How could you handle it?

44. We were thinking of an older/younger person for this job.
45. You are overqualified for this position, aren't you?
46. What are your financial needs?
47. What is the minimum salary you would accept?
48. What is your salary history?
49. Are there any questions you would like to ask about the job/company?
50. We have all the information we need. We'll be in touch with you.
51. We don't feel that you have what we are looking for.
52. Tell me about yourself.
53. How long have you been looking for a new position?
54. Why are you considering leaving your current position?
55. What did you wish to accomplish in your current job, but were unable to do? Why?
56. What will your current supervisor say about your performance (or most recent pat supervisor)?
57. What will your colleagues say about you?
58. How would your subordinates describe you?
59. What did your most recent performance appraisal say about the quality of your performance?
60. Have you ever been fired or resigned from a position?
61. What is the greatest value you bring to this organization?
62. What are your immediate, five-year and 10-year goals?
63. Define your leadership and management style?
64. Define your decision-making style?
65. Define your success in problem solving?
66. Tell me about your communication skills?
67. Tell me about your negotiation skills?
68. What systems and software do you know?
69. What are the greatest contributors to your success?
70. How do you deal with stressful situations? (Describe a highly stressful situation you experienced at work within the past 12 months and how you handled it.)
71. What is the #1 achievement of your career?
72. What are the top five contributions you have made during your career?

73. What are your greatest strengths?
74. What are your limitations?
75. What motivates you to perform and excel?
76. Do you consider yourself a leader or a follower?
77. Are you a risk taker?
78. How do you determine or evaluate success?
79. What is the worst mistake you ever made on the job and how did you remedy the situation?
80. What have you learned from your mistakes?
81. If you could change something about your life, what would it be and why?
82. What are your views on continuing education? For yourself? For your employees?
83. Who was your most valuable mentor and why?
84. When you are hiring, what do you look for as the most important attribute in a candidate?
85. Have you ever had a supervisor you did not get along with and how did you manage the relationship?
86. Have you ever had to fire someone for poor performance? How did you manage the situation?
87. What are you looking for in a new opportunity?
88. How would you describe your ideal position?
89. What other positions are you interviewing for?
90. Is job security a prime consideration for you?
91. How long do you expect to stay with our company?
92. Suppose that we were to offer you the position today. If you could have only two other employees working with you to build this company, what would those individuals be responsible for and why?
93. What will you bring to this position that another candidate will not?
94. Are you willing to travel? How often?
95. What is your expectation for number of hours to be worked each week?
96. Why are you interested in our company?
97. What type of person would you hire for this position?
98. Why should we hire you?
99. What are your compensation requirements?

Chapter 10 – Ask the Right Questions

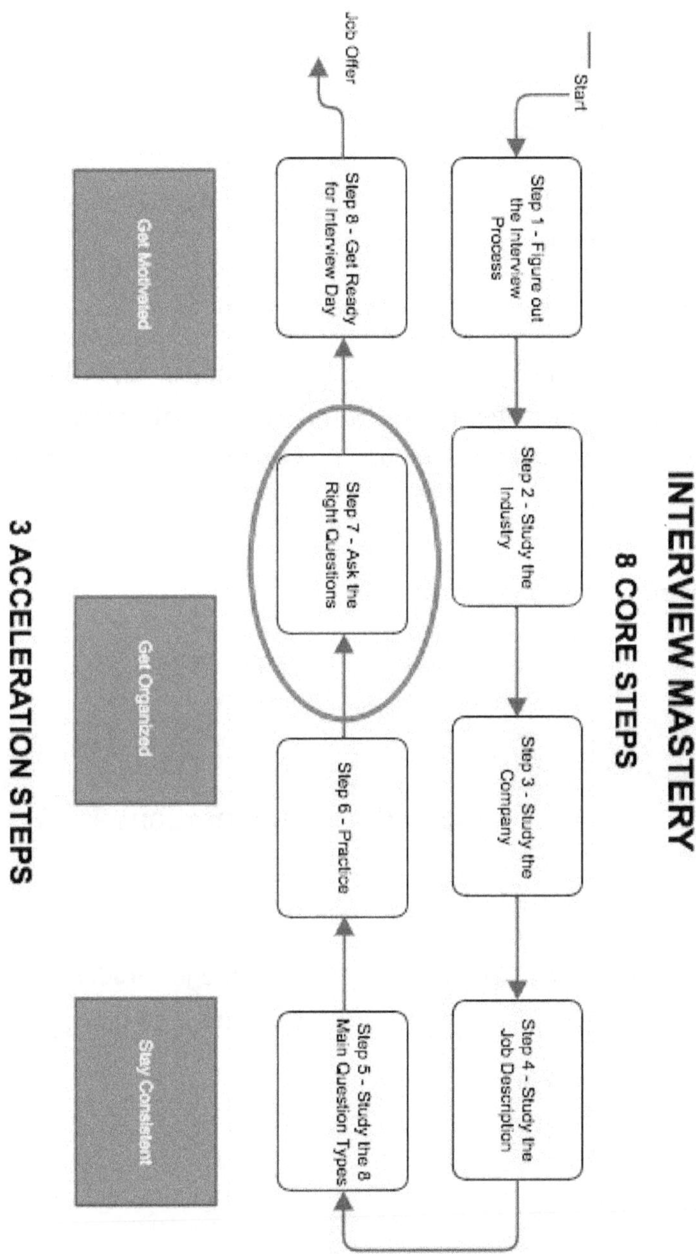

Figure 37 – The 8 x 3 Interview Mastery Framework – Step 7

You might think that you've done everything to prepare for your interview. But you have one more step to prepare for: Questions.

Now it's your turn to ask your interviewers questions.

DO NOT IGNORE THIS STEP.

This is chance for you to showcase to your interviewer your passion for the job and the company.

Interviewers are judging you based on the questions you ask

You might think that the interview is over when the interviewer asks – "Do you have any questions for me?". The truth of the matter is that it is not. This is your chance to leave your interviewer with a lasting impression.

How?

By asking some good questions.

Let's look at a framework next about asking questions.

Framework to ask Questions

We will go back at this point of time to our old friend – **ICJC.** Remember ICJC from step 5. I – Industry, C – Company, J – Job, C – Culture. We'll use the same framework here.

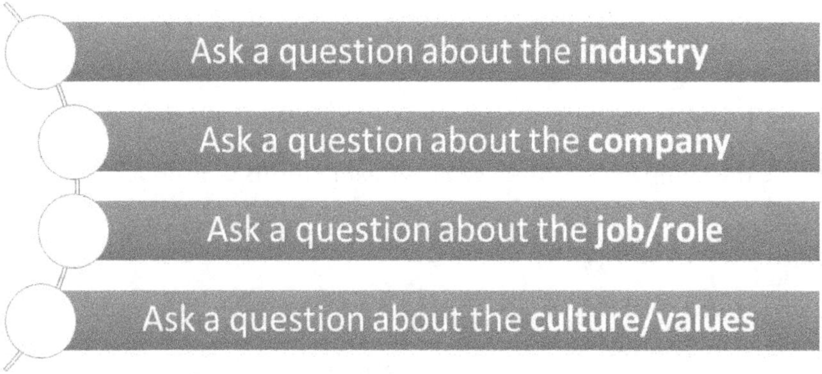

Ask a question about the **industry**

Ask a question about the **company**

Ask a question about the **job/role**

Ask a question about the **culture/values**

Figure 38 – ICJC Framework to Ask Questions

You can do this for each interviewer you meet during the entire process.

My Favorites List

The following is a list of questions I ask time and time again in interviews and it has always worked. Use this as a set of examples to apply to your upcoming interview.

Example Question - Industry

How do you think the industry has changed over the years and what do you think is the outlook for the industry?

Example Question – Company

What's the company's future? What's next in terms of products/services and/or growth?

Example Question - Job/Role

What are the top challenges for this role as of today? How do you see this role solving those challenges?

Or

What's the long-term career path for this role?

Example Question - Culture/Values

How would you describe the company's culture? How do teams operate and make decisions on a day to day basis?

Do not ask these questions

There are three categories of questions you shouldn't ask:

1. **Red Flag Questions -** Anything around salary, vacation, benefits etc.

Even though you don't mean to, this might come across in the wrong way.

2. **Obvious Questions** – Do not ask questions that you should know answers to already.

For example: How do you make money as a company? This might show that you just didn't prepare.

3. **Critical Questions** – Finally anything that criticizes the company/group/person for making a certain decision.

Example: Why didn't you follow a strategy like Y? You might come across as Mr. Smarty Pants.

Homework

As part of this book, please use the "Questions to Ask" worksheet to come up with questions that make sense based on the information in this chapter. You can also use from a list of questions that we've already provided.

Questions to Ask Worksheet

1. **Company Name: __________________________________**

2. **Industry Related Questions**

____

____

____

____

3. **Company Related Questions**

____

____

____

____

4. **Job/Role Related Questions**

____

____

____

____

5. Culture/Values Related Questions

Questions to Ask – Use for Interviews

Question

Question

Question

Question

Question

____

____

____

Question

____

____

____

Great Questions You Can Ask in an Interview

Position Description

1. Would you describe the key responsibilities of the position for me, please? Can you describe the activities that go on in (my area of interest)? Are there any other assignments not specifically mentioned in the position description?
2. To whom would I be reporting (what department)? Can you tell me about the people who would be reporting to me?
3. Is this a newly created position? If not, how long did the previous person hold it? Was the previous person promoted?
4. What skills and characteristics are considered the most useful for success in the job I'm applying for?
5. Could you describe a typical day?

Judgment Questions for the Interviewer

1. What kind of personal attributes and qualifications does your company value?
2. What is the most significant challenge facing your staff now?
3. What have been some of the best results/accomplishments produced by people in this position?
4. What are your projections for this department/position for the next year? (Specify type of projections, e.g., sales, production, products, profits, etc.). What are your

plans for expanding (sales, audit, research, or whatever) department?

5. What do you see ahead for your company in the next five years?
6. How do you rate your competition?

Education & Professional Development

1. What additional training might be necessary for this position?
2. Are there training programs available to me so that I can learn and grow professionally?
3. Does the firm support further college education for its employees?
4. What is the company's position on participating in professional organizations?

Company Information

1. What are some of the major short-and-long-range goals that the company has?
2. What are two or three characteristics that the company considers to be unique or attractive about it?
3. What are some of the common denominators among the most successful employees?

Career Paths

1. Assuming I was hired and performed well for several years, what additional opportunities might this job lead

to? Can you tell me about the career path this position offers?

2. Could you tell me about the people who have preceded me in this position and in the department? Where are they now, and what are they doing?
3. Is it your usual policy to promote from within?
4. Does advancement to upper management require an advanced degree?

At the End of the Interview

1. Based on our meeting today, do you believe I am a fit for this position?
2. I'd really like to work for your firm. I think it's a great company and I'm confident I could do this job well. Can you describe the hiring process? What's the next step for selection process? When do you expect to make a hiring decision for this position? When can I get back to you?

Chapter 11 – Step 8 - Get Ready for Interview Day

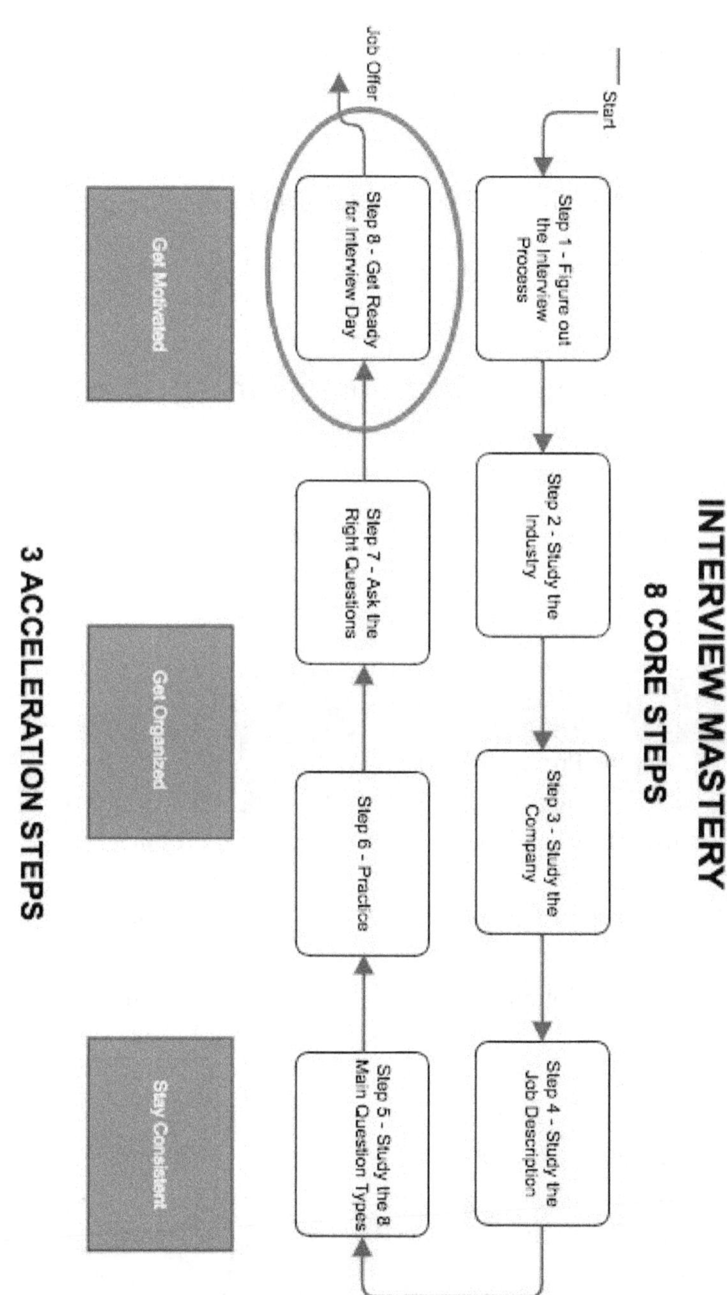

Figure 39 – The 8 x 3 Interview Mastery Framework – Step 8

Great job so far. You've done some amazing work so far. By now you should be well prepared to absolutely ace your interview.

However, there are a few more steps that you should do before you go in to that big day. That's what this chapter is all about. It's about preparing you for your interview day or I day.

First things first let's look at a preparation plan for your upcoming interview.

Preparation Plan for Your Initial Screens

Below is a preparation plan for your initial screens.

Area of Studying	Approximate Time to Spend
Interview Process	1 hour
Industry Information	1 hour
Company Information	1 – 2 hours
Job Description	1 hour
Main Question Types and Stories	5 – 7 hours
Practice Question Types	5 hours
Ask Questions	1 hour
Prep for Interview (Resume, Cheat	1 hour

Sheets etc.)	
Total	16 – 19 hours

The bulk of your time should be spent on the main question types and practice for this interview. We recommend a total of 16 - 19 hours of studying for this interview, so definitely plan accordingly.

Please note that you might have at least two phone screens, so that's why the additional time in preparing for them.

Preparation Plan for Your Onsite Interviews

The good news is that if you spend enough time during your phone preparation, the onsite interviews should be a breeze.

Below is a preparation calendar for the onsite interview.

Area of Studying	Approximate Time to Spend
Industry Information	1 - 2 hours
Company Information	1 – 2 hours
Job Description	1 hour
Main Question Types and Stories	10 hours
Practice Question Types	10 hours

Ask Questions	1 hour
Prep for Interview (Resume, Cheat Sheets etc.)	1 hour
Total	25 – 27 hours

We recommend a total of 25 - 27 hours of preparation. I know this might sound a lot, but remember that this is a one-time activity that you will be performing.

This is the time to go all in. It's time to prepare yourself for your big day. Remember this:

You are putting in all this effort for your big game that is going to last five hours or so.

Crazy right! That's all it takes. Five hours of your life to a dream job. Why not go all in? I'm sure you can sacrifice 20-25 hours of a week preparing for a five-hour interview. This is your time to give your absolute best.

Supplementary Tools

Then in addition to your preparation calendar, there are a few more tools that I recommend you use before your big day.

I believe that these tools are necessary to hold with you at every given point of time during the entire interview process.

These tools will take you to the next level as compared to every candidate out there.

Figure 40 – 6 Supplementary Tools

1. Resume

The Resume is Important

As much as my personal view is that it is very hard to summarize what a person can bring to the table on a single page, the resume unfortunately is the first step in the job search process, so ensuring that you get it right is extremely important.

Resume Template

As part of this book, I've provided for you a resume template that you can use as part of your job search.

It's a template that top notch business schools prescribe to their students.

We firmly believe it will help you stand apart from the crowd. Please use the resume template from this book.

Download Link – http://passdropit.com/dmybnylu

Password - k88sz3c024feq

2. Online Profile (s)

Two words

Scrub It

Currently, whether you like it or not, whether you believe it or not, your online profile plays a big role in getting you a job or not. And I don't just mean this for professional social media sites like LinkedIn, but any presence you have out there will be looked at.

Employers can get turned on or off by your profile based on what you have on it, so. Please make sure your online profiles are clean before you begin your job search.

For Every Social Media Profile...

Use a professional photograph

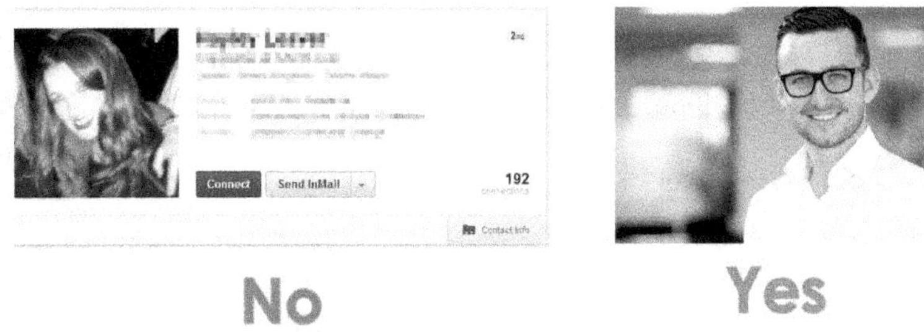

Figure 41 – LinkedIn Picture

Additionally,

For every post and/or image you have out there:

1. Remove any references to sexuality.
2. Remove any references to guns, violence, or drugs.
3. Remove any references to profanity.
4. Check your spellings and grammar – make sure everything is correct.

We understand that this might be you and you might be unwilling to change, however, do note that employers consistently look for this information, so it's worth your time cleaning your profile up before you begin the search. It will only help you convert better.

For LinkedIn, especially, please make sure that your entire profile is complete. This means, put every detail of your resume out on the profile. LinkedIn is nothing but your resume online.

Experience

Chief Operating Officer (COO)
Unikrn
January 2015 – Present (1 year 9 months) | Greater Seattle Area

Strategy – Working with the management team on Unikrn's strategic plan and defining and executing on Unikrn's goals by aligning people, plans and processes around a shared purpose.

Global Expansion - Successfully expanded Unikrn's business to UK and Australia. On track to add 3 more countries by Q3 2016.

Operations – Defining systems, tools, controls, processes and milestones cross functionally at Unikrn and leading and aligning all global teams to execute on defined business objectives and targets for 2015/2016.

Budgeting and Financial Planning – Managing budget ($10MM), P&L, financial projections, due diligence and ROI analysis for all initiatives at Unikrn and managing portfolio of associated projects. Successfully took the company to a $7MM Series A raise.

Team Leadership – Successfully evolved the global organization from 5 to 40 employees. Direct reports include 3 VPs and 2 Directors. Built and run teams in Seattle, Sydney, Berlin, Croatia and India.

Chief Executive Officer (CEO) and Principal Consultant
Starterz.co
July 2016 – Present (3 months) | Greater Seattle Area

Starterz is a boutique management consulting firm, specifically focused on startups and small businesses, advising them on business, technology and capital raising.

As CEO and Co-Founder, I run all functional areas of the business - Product, Marketing, Consulting, Finance and Administration.

Director of Program Management and Operations
Techstars
March 2014 – December 2014 (10 months) | Greater Chicago Area

Program Director - Established new and maintained existing strategic partnerships with CEOs,

Figure 42 – LinkedIn Sample

Additionally, update all other profiles.

This includes Twitter, snapchat, Facebook, Google+ and others. Please do not think that employers will not look at other profiles.

In today's day and age, you are out in the open, whether you like it or not.

3. Worksheets/Cheat sheets

As part of this book, you will get several different worksheets that you will need to fill in as you are doing your preparation. We highly recommend that you take the time to fill these sheets in as you start your interview preparation.

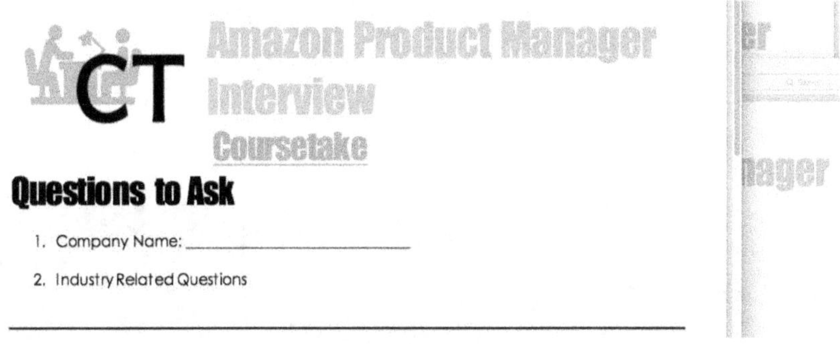

Figure 43 – Cheat sheets

For Phone Interviews, Only

Another very important tip is to fill in your interview sheets and keep them handy when you are doing your phone interviews.

Use these as cheat sheets while answering.

This will ensure that you don't forget anything you've learnt and give you an opportunity to showcase your confidence during your interview process.

Note: Please do not keep your cheat sheets out when on a video conference or onsite. It's a sign of lack of preparation.

4. Portfolio

In today's day and age, it's not only your work experience that matters, but your portfolio is extremely important too.

A portfolio will help you stand apart from the crowd and absolutely impress your future employer.

What do I mean by portfolio?

Here is a list:

Examples:
Presentations that you have done.
Blog articles that you have written.
Business Plans that you have created.
Software Development – Code Samples.
Design Work e.g. illustrations, web pages, mobile pages etc. etc.
Any personal websites or projects you have run.
Product Plans
College Projects

Figure 44 – Portfolio Examples

These are just samples. Whatever your profile is, find work from your past that you can showcase to your employer and impress them.

Where do I place these documents?

You can place these documents on your own personal website if you have one. Additionally, your LinkedIn profile also gives you the opportunity to write blog posts, upload documents etc. Specific job profiles will have certain online tools that the community uses. E.g. Designers use Dribble, Developers use GitHub.

So, make sure your profile is online, current and accurate on these places. Employers will be expecting to see these.

5. Appearance

What to wear during an interview?

We have one rule of thumb when it comes to dressing up for interviewers – "Always Overdress than Underdress".

When in doubt, better to dress up in business formals.

If you're male, this means a suit and tie – and not something that looks like a hand-me-down from your older brother.

You don't need to spend a fortune on a suit, but it's worth getting at least a moderately priced one that fits you well and that implies that you're taking the interview seriously.

Figure 45 – Business Formals (Male)

If you're female, "business formal" also means "wear a suit" – do not wear a dress or go in looking like you're auditioning to be a pole dancer.

Figure 46 – Business Formals (Female)

On Interview Day – What to Bring with you?

Just bring a nice-looking folder with hard copies of your resume/CV, a few extra sheets of paper, and a pen or pencil (in case you get questions where you need to write something down).

If you have a printable portfolio, make sure to carry that with you or an iPad/laptop if you need to show your portfolio to the hiring team.

6. Confidence

This should've been the first chapter of this book.

Look, we've already explained to you before that the entire job search process is a game of numbers. There are absolutely no emotions that should be attached to the process. The more you attach emptions to the process, you more you are going to be worried, or scared or think – "What if I don't get the job?", or "What if I don't make it"?

All this is just going to decrease your confidence. I hope I have convinced so far through this book that:

Confidence is all that matters.

At the end of the day, my friends, you can study all you want, you can practice all the questions you want, but if you can't walk into that room and talk like you own that room, you are not going to get the job.

So, you've got to practice, practice and practice.

And what if you don't get the job?

Well, simple – move on. Open you're the next opportunity in your recruiting pipeline and get moving. Open your calendar and schedule more study sessions, application sessions and continue the process.

So how do I increase my confidence?

Firstly, please do all the exercises in this class. Please do not skimp on them. Please do them seriously. They are in here because they work.

Secondly, get your mind right during the interview process – exercise daily, meditate for a period, eat healthy. Follow everything I've taught you in the appendices and the three acceleration steps, especially the first one – "Get Motivated".

Its these little things will help increase your confidence, make you look and feel confident and good.

Thirdly, Have fun. This can be a stressful time. Go out, network with others, have a good time with your friends. Don't take the entire process so seriously. Make it part of your daily routine.

Homework

As part of your homework, before your interview, use the interview day checklist to ensure that you've got all the pieces together before your interview.

Interview Day Checklist

Grooming done?

- ☐ Outfit?
- ☐ Perfume?
- ☐ Hair?
- ☐ Makeup?
- ☐ Shoes?

Folder Ready?

- ☐ Professional looking folder?
- ☐ Resume copies?
- ☐ Cover letter copies?
- ☐ Business cards?
- ☐ Pen?
- ☐ Notebook?
- ☐ List of questions?
- ☐ Portfolio (if any)?
- ☐ Cheat sheets?

Social Media Scrubbed?

- ☐ LinkedIn up to date?
- ☐ Facebook clean?
- ☐ Twitter clean?
- ☐ Google+ clean?
- ☐ Other Social Profiles?
- ☐ Website up to date (if any?)

Confidence Check?

- ☐ Feeling motivated?

Chapter 12 – Follow Up

Right after your interview, you'll want to follow up with your interviewers immediately. This follow up must be done the night after your interview or in the worst case a day later.

Decisions for interviews are made fast, so you will want to use this opportunity to showcase your strengths once again, motivations and fit to your future employer.

The biggest advantage of following up is that in the worst case that you had a bad interview with one of your interviewers, this will give you an opportunity to correct that mistake by a good follow up letter. If the interviewer was on the fence, you have one final opportunity to convert his or her "maybe" to a "yes".

Homework

Please use the template as part of this book to send thank you letters to your interviewers. You will want to send one letter per interviewer.

Thank You Letter Template

Your street address
Your City, State, and Zip Code

Date of the letter

Name of the Recipient
Job Title of the Recipient
Name of the Employer
Employer's Street Address
Employer's City, State, and Zip Code

Dear Mr./Ms. Last Name:

Thank you very much for the opportunity to interview for the position of [job title] yesterday [or today, if appropriate]. I enjoyed speaking with you, meeting other members of the staff, and the opportunity to learn more about this position. I am very interested in this position and the opportunity to join your team.

This job feels like a very good match between my skills and experience and the requirements of this job. As we discussed, you need someone with strong [whatever] skills, and I have extensive experience with [whatever technology or tool that is important to the job and that you have experience using]. In addition, in my current [or former] job as [names or type of employer in your past] has provided the opportunity to polish my skills in [whatever] and [whatever] needed for your [job title] position.

Again, thank you for considering me for this wonderful opportunity. Please let me know if you have any questions or concerns or need more information. I look forward to hearing from you next week [or whenever they said they would be in touch] and hope to join your staff soon.

Best regards,

[your name]
[Your tagline, like Customer Support Specialist"]
[Your job search email address]

Chapter 13 – Last Minute Interview Tips and Tricks

In this final chapter before the conclusion, I'd like to give you a few last-minute tips and tricks to help you ace your upcoming interview.

Body Language During Your Interview

When talking to your interviewer, look them straight into the eye. Failure to look in the eye indicates that you have something to hide from them. Don't make this mistake.

Greeting

When you meet your interviewer for the first time, greet them with a firm handshake, face him or her, sit straight up, and, of course, look them in the eye.

Enthusiastic, but NOT Aggressive

You want to be excited about what the company does, so sighing, looking out of the window, or checking your watch during a question will not create the right impression.

You want to come across as confident, enthusiastic, and cheerful.

Avoid Being Defensive

Avoid being defensive. Sweating or changing the topic is not going to take you too far.

Make each minute of the interview a positive experience. Introducing negativity is surely going to dim your chances.

Lying During Your Interview

In short, don't. You will get caught.

Employers check references and they do background checks. If you are caught lying, NOT only will you be embarrassed, you will significantly increase your chances of dismissal.

At the same time, it is NOT necessary to share anything and everything.

How to Ace Any Interview?

If you remember, we started off our conversation with a simple "Strengths", "Motivation" and "Fit" framework to ace your upcoming interview. I said that you will need to consistently demonstrate your strengths, motivation and fit to your employer.

Now I'm going to add onto that three more things your future employer cares about, specifically your hiring manager.

1. Will you take the job if I offer it to you?
2. Will you make me look like a genius for recommending you.
3. What are you going to cost me?

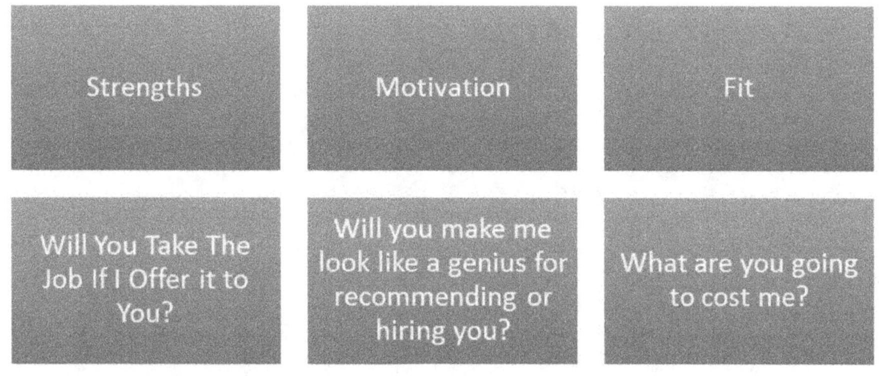

Figure 47 – How to Ace Any Interview?

Keep this list in mind as you go through the entire interview process. Keep in mind that the hiring team is consistently looking for these six key points.

Chapter 14 - Conclusion

This short chapter here is really meant to give you one piece of advice before your upcoming interview.

Don't Expect Anything

Going into the interview, just remember that the company needs you – it's not the other way around.

Remember that there are many opportunities out there.

Job searching is nothing but a game of numbers. The more you apply, the more your chances are to succeed.

Remember our salesman analogy. You must consistently look for clients and do not get attached to one company. Keep shopping around and sell your services. Get into "sales" mode. Then once you are done selling and you have multiple offers in hand, then the tables will be turned. Then it's your turn to buy.

Just remember that I've laid an entire plan for you and all you need to do is "Follow the Plan". Keep following through day in and day out and success will be by your side.

With I'd like to congratulate you on completing this book. I have no doubt that you will be able to ace the interview process at your target company.

If you need any extra help, please email me at any given point of time and I will be more than happy to help you. I'm available anytime at kunal@coursetake.com.

Appendix A – The Career Planning Mastery Framework

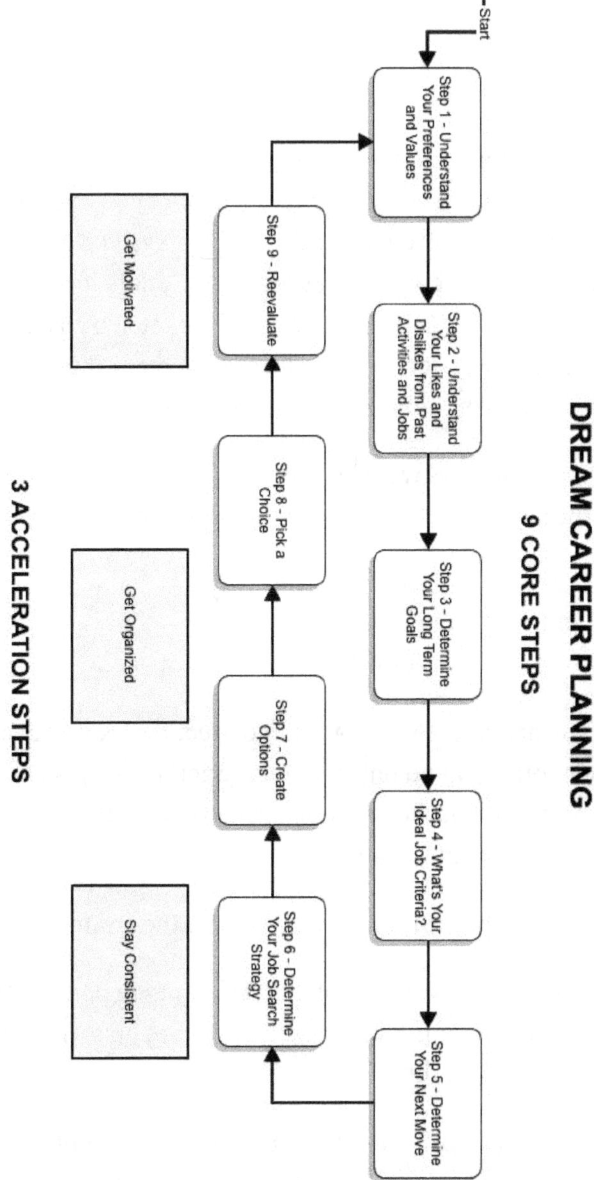

Figure 48 – The Career Planning Mastery Framework

In this chapter, we're going to start focusing on step 1 of our 5-step dream career blueprint. If you remember from chapter 1, step 1 was called "Create a Career Plan" and in this chapter, I'm going to put together a complete framework for you to start thinking about your career aka your career plan.

But I'd like to take you through a slight detour first.

Imagine for a moment that you an organization. The main goal of an organization is to make a profit. To make a profit and grow your business, you would probably want to put together a strategy in place. This strategy would include defining your vision as a company, defining your mission as a company, your values, understanding the market and customers that you want to go after, understanding the environment that you operate it, understanding your competition and much more.

You, like other companies would do something known as the "Strategic Planning" process, where they answer three high level questions:

1. Where are you now as a company?
2. Where do you want to be?
3. How will you get there?

It's from this strategic analysis that you conduct that will you put together goals for your company and only then put together the plan to execute on those goals. In short, you wouldn't blindly execute without keeping the big picture at the back of your head.

The operations for your company would follow the strategy.

Once you have a clear strategy in place, you can then operate the company, launch programs and projects, recruit people, monitor metrics, put budgets in place, etc. etc.

Additionally, you will most likely come back to your strategy and operations each year to check how you did against your plan, continue to set new goals for the new year and grow your business.

So, if companies can put in so much effort to ensure that they have a strategy in place before they execute, why don't we as individuals have our own career strategy in place before we find our next job?

Additionally, why don't we do a gut check each year on our own careers and figure out how we're measuring against our plan?

Most people look for "jobs". They don't seek "careers". I urge you to think differently. If you want to take your career to the next level; if you want to find your dream opportunity and if you want to get to executive status in your career as soon as possible, then don't find your next job before you put together your career plan.

A job is nothing but a short term tactical move that will give you short term benefits, but will not give you a long-term career.

"Career Planning" is what six and seven figure executives do year after year in their careers to ensure that they can accelerate their careers FAST. If things are NOT according to plan, they make changes FAST. Today is your opportunity to follow the same strategies as six and seven figure executives and it starts with the career planning process.

Mission, Vision, and Values (MVV)

Companies' start their strategic planning process by defining their MVV; i.e. their **Vision (V), their Values (V) and Mission (M)**.

Let's define what these mean first:

Vision – A company's vision is its long-term dream. It's the north star that the company is going after.

Mission – A company's mission is its current task at hand to achieve that vision.

Values – Values are the rules by which decisions are made on a day to day basis.

We'll use this framework to develop the high-level career plan for our lives.

Let's now discuss how to map your career plan to this mission, vision, and values framework. This entire process is summarized in Figure 49.

Vision

The first step of the career planning process is to define the vision for your life. This is done by doing two important steps.

1. Defining your long-term goals.
2. Defining your ideal job criteria.

Both these steps take you into dreamland and give you the opportunity to idealize your ultimate career move and the ideal job you would love to have.

Once you have this defined is when you can now move onto figuring out your values as an individual.

Values

The second step of the career planning process is to define your values as an individual. This again consists of two steps.

1. Define your preferences as an individual; i.e. the way you behave, the way you relate to others, the way you make decisions, your preferences in terms of office environment etc. etc. These are elements of the culture that you will fit into well.

2. Think about all the activities that you do and determine what are your likes and dislikes. People tend to do the things that they like well, so finding a career that can accentuate these strengths will get you closer to your vision faster.

1 is about culture and 2 is about your strengths and weaknesses.

Once you have your vision and values in place, it's time to move onto your mission; i.e. the next move that will take you closer to your vision.

Mission

Your mission is now all about finding that next move that aligns with your vision and your values as a person.

You start by following the right job search strategy to interview with multiple places. Yes, you heard that right. You've got to find jobs in such a way that you have multiple interviews lined up. Then you ace those interviews, get multiple job offers and pick one that aligns with the vision for your career and your values.

This is accomplished by following steps 2, 3 and 4 of the 5-step dream career blueprint.

The 9 x 3 Career Planning Blueprint

This brings us to the 9 x 3 Career Planning Blueprint that is summarized in Figure 48. The entire Mission, Vision and Values framework is summarized as nine core steps and three acceleration steps that you need to consistently follow to achieve that dream career.

1. **Step 1** – Understand your preferences
2. **Step 2** – Understand your likes and dislikes

3. **Step 3** – Determine your long-term goals
4. **Step 4** – Determine your ideal job criteria
5. **Step 5** – Determine your next move
6. **Step 6** – Pick your job search strategy
7. **Step 7** – Create options; i.e. multiple job offers
8. **Step 8** – Pick a choice
9. **Step 9** – Repeat each year

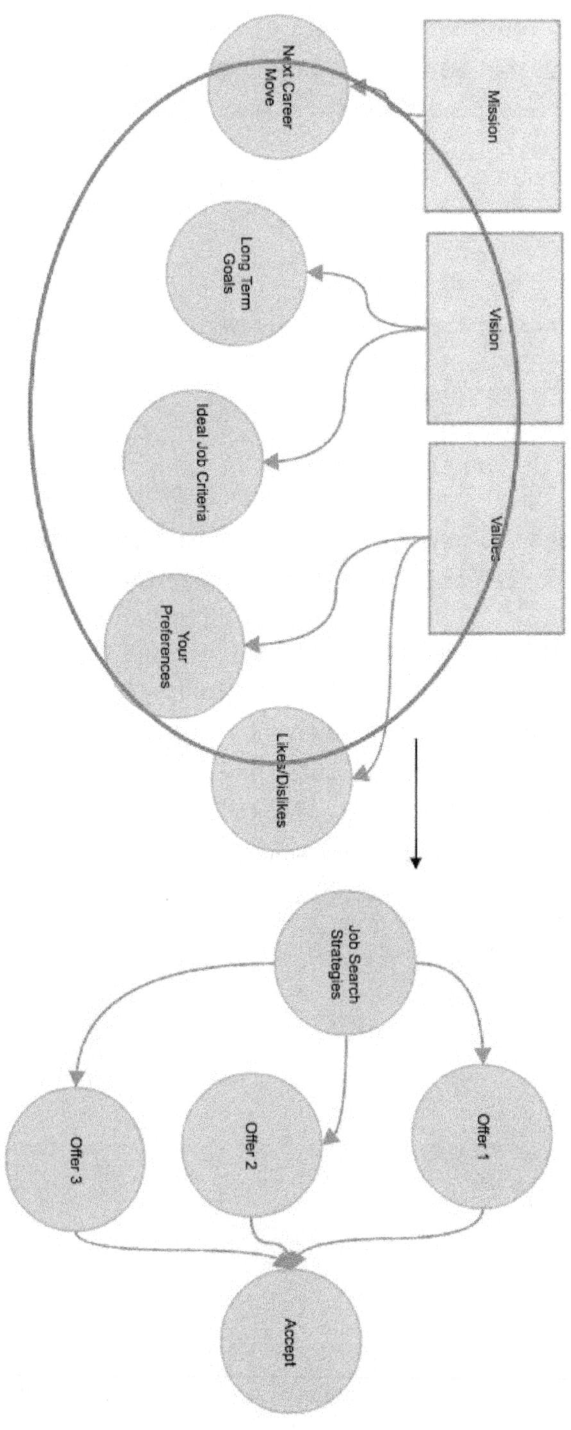

Figure 49 – The MVV Framework as Applied to Your Career

Don't forget to consistently do step 9 each year – reevaluate. Remember the three things that companies do each year to grow their business. They answer the three important questions each year:

1. Where are you now as a company?
2. Where do you want to be?
3. How will you get there?

You too must answer the same three questions as an individual.

1. Where are you now in your career?
2. Where do you want to be?
3. How do you plan to get there?

It's only through this constant introspection each year that you will be able to take your career from "average" to "executive".

But following the nine steps is not enough. Remember the three acceleration steps from chapter 2 and appendices E, G, and F. If you want to truly accelerate your career, you will have to get motivated about this process, you will have to get organized and you will have to be consistent. Apply these three acceleration steps to the nine core career planning steps and see your career accelerate in no time.

Appendix B – Job Search Mastery Framework

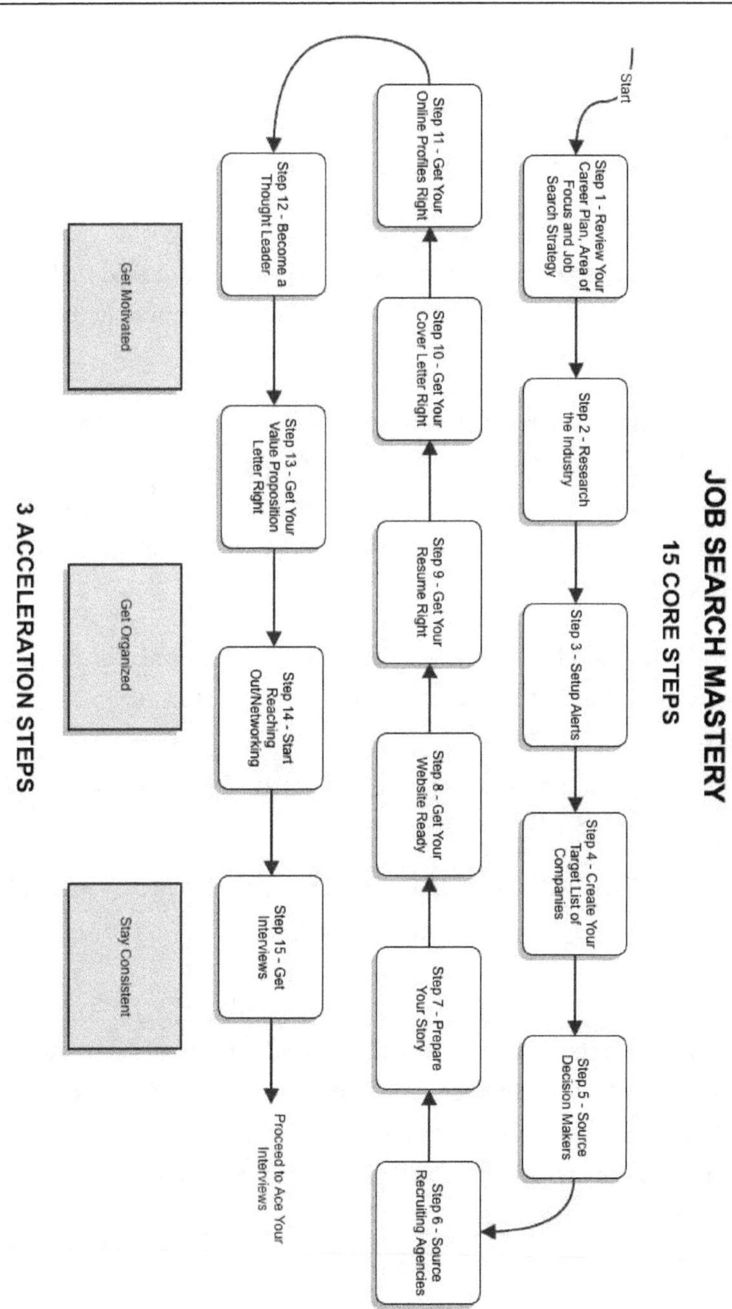

Figure 50 – The Job Search Mastery Framework

In this chapter, I'd like to lay out a framework for the job search process. Specifically, I'd like to list out 15 steps that if you start following, I believe you should start seeing success right away.

A few questions to get started:

Have you ever felt that you have been stuck in a job rut in your life, doing the same things again and again and not knowing where your career is going?

Have you ever tried to make a change, tried applying to several jobs online, possibly tried to reach out to people on LinkedIn only to never hear back?

Have you wondered why there are some folks who are able to take their careers all the way to the "next level" becoming executives and getting promotion after promotion regularly and then there are some others who are pretty much stuck in a job rut, only going to work for the sake of a paycheck?

If you fall into one of these categories then this chapter is for you. So, with that background out of the way, let's get directly into your job search strategy.

The Inbound Outbound Job Search Strategy Organized into 15 Steps

I've created something known as the inbound outbound strategy, that lays out a framework with specific steps that you can do to find a job in today's market. Once we go through the inbound outbound strategy, I'll talk about how the strategy is organized into 15 steps that you can start applying one after the other immediately.

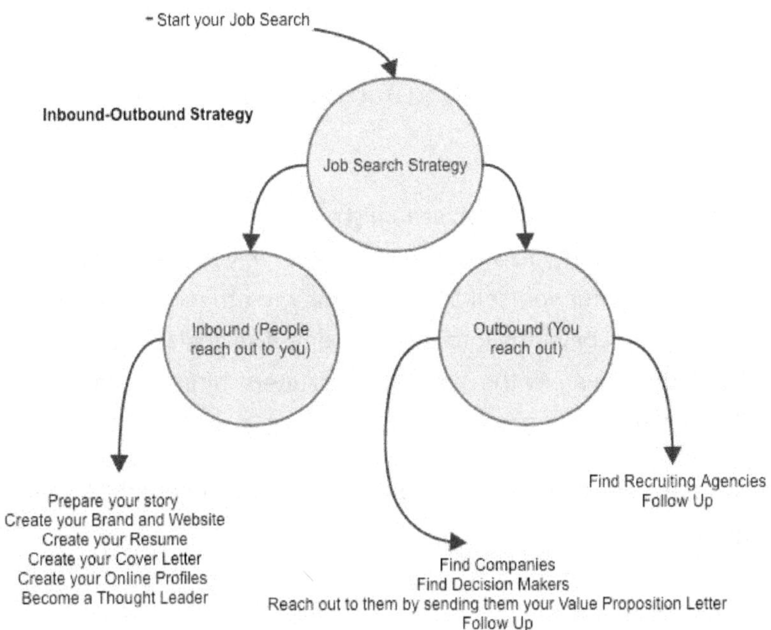

Figure 51 – The Inbound Outbound Job Search Strategy

To find a job in today's market, I recommend considering two high level strategies.

a. **Inbound** – This strategy involves creating your profiles and positioning yourself in a way that you can be sought after when it comes to the job search process. This means hiring managers seek you, recruiters seek you, recruiting agencies seek you.

b. **Outbound** – This strategy involves you finding companies, decision makers, opportunities and taking control of the job search process in your own hands.

If these two strategies are combined, both effects work together in unison and opportunities start coming by your desk. It is then your job to convert those opportunities into real job offers. Let's look at these two strategies in detail now.

The Inbound Job Search Strategy

As a reminder, the Inbound job search strategy is all about you positioning yourself in a way that you are a thought leader in your field. You create a brand and a story for yourself that will signify to others that you are the person we should be hiring into the company. The goal is to get sought after by all the players in the industry – recruiters, hiring managers, recruiting agencies.

Here are the steps you should do to execute on the inbound job search strategy.

START BY "PREPARING YOUR STORY"

Your story consists of the following:

a. Where are you today?
b. Where do you want to go?
c. What have you done so far to take you from where you are to where you want to go?
d. What value can you add/Why you?

Students and Professionals ready to get back into the job market, should be crystal-clear on their story. This requires some reflection on your part to answer the three questions I've outlined here. But once these questions are answered and you are clear on your career path, the conversation gets a lot easier.

DELIVER YOUR STORY IN PERSON

Once you have your story prepared you need to be ready to deliver your story. This is the elevator pitch of the four questions that you should've already answered. Prepare two versions of your delivery – one a two-minute version and the other a 30 second version where you can outline the four points discussed in this section. Your story is key as you start the job search process. Your story is a great conversation starter, specifically with hiring managers as it clearly not only talks about YOU, but also what YOU can bring to the organization.

Note that the delivery of the story here is different from when you asked about the same question in the interview process. There is a different format when discussing your story in the interview process, which we will discuss in other blog posts.

DELIVER YOUR STORY IN OTHER FORMATS

Now that you have your story, it's time to deliver your story in other formats namely your resume, your website, your LinkedIn profile, your cover letter etc. etc. Note how this is different from how we normally think about all these different platforms. At the end of the day, all these platforms say the same thing – your story, but they say it differently.

When I read your resume, I should still be able to get answers to the same four questions discussed in this post, however the format of delivery is different. The same is the case with your cover letter or your LinkedIn profile. Anyone reading it should be crystal-clear on where you are now, where you want to go, what have you done so far to bring you to where you are and what value you can add to your future organization.

CREATE YOUR WEBSITE

A great way for you to be sought after regularly is by creating and maintaining your website. Through a website, you can showcase your work, your brand, and give answers to the four questions as part of your story with ease. A website is like an automated recruiting machine. That combined with step # 4 – Become a Thought Leader, can certainly accentuate your results of getting opportunities by your plate.

CREATE YOUR LINKEDIN PROFILE

Next is to create a strong LinkedIn profile. This is another avenue that can be used to tell your story. However, the difference here is that your story can be a lot more aspirational as compared to your resume. Additionally, it can be written in the first person and there is no length constraint as compared to a resume. Also, you can take advantage of having a strong summary statement describing your story in detail. An important point for your LinkedIn profile is to ensure that you have all portions of it complete and professionally done to ensure that you show up in all relevant searches for the position you are looking to get into.

CREATE YOUR RESUME

Then comes your resume – another platform to deliver your story. The difference between a resume and other formats is exactly that – It has a certain format that you'll need to adhere to. The basic format for each bullet in your resume should be as follows:

What did you achieve? The actual outcome of your work.

How did you achieve it? The process you used to achieve it.

A big mistake that candidates make as part of their resume is that it is normally backward looking and not forward looking. I ready tons of resumes everyday as part of my job as a hiring manager and the theme is consistent. I don't know where do you want to go and what value you can add my organization. That's exactly what I seek – Why you? How can you help me solve my organization's problems?

The second mistake that candidates make is that fail to highlight the outcome of their work. Did you reduce costs, did you increase revenues, did you save time, did you improve quality, did you improve efficiency? As a hiring manager, I do care about what you did, but only after I know what results you achieved. The results you achieved in your previous organization is an indicator to me that you will be able to achieve similar results for my organization. Thereby, indicating to me the value you can bring me.

CREATE YOUR COVER LETTER

Now it's time for your cover letter. Think about the cover letter in the same light as your story. It is once again only a different format to say the same thing. The cover letter should also contain the same components of your story, however here is a format that I recommend.

The Introductory paragraph - Introduce yourself and create a compelling hook

The Middle paragraph(s) - Target the letter to the company and the job

The Closing paragraph – Create a call to action

Use this format, but remember that your story needs to come out clearly as part of the cover letter too. In fact, when the cover letter is used in combination with the resume, your website, and other online profiles, you are still stating your story, but now in different ways – some formal, some informal, but the reader or the listener should get a clear sense of who you are, what value you can add and what you can bring to the table.

CREATE OTHER ONLINE PROFILES

A big mistake many candidates make is to think that they have a professional brand and a separate personal brand. This in my opinion is incorrect. At the end of the day, your brand is your brand. This is clearly seen when you have a professional LinkedIn profile, but an extremely unprofessional Twitter or Facebook profile. One suggestion I would make is that when you are going through the job search process, do make sure that all your profiles are professionally maintained.

This means removing any posts or videos that might raise red flags – related to profanity, nudity, foul language, or anything else that might cause your future employer to raise his or her eyebrow.

BECOME A THOUGHT LEADER

4 is all about thought leadership. I believe this is extremely important in today's day and age, a day and age that is social in nature, a day and age that is global, virtual, and becoming more and more competitive. What does thought leadership really mean? Thought leadership is nothing but "Putting content out there regularly that relates to your future industry, position and/or companies". This content could take several forms. Here are examples of how you can put yourself out there a lot more:

Start by becoming an expert – which means start reading books, take certifications, do more courses and/or online trainings in your field.

Then create your own perspective on your topics and publish content. You can use the following platforms to publish your content:

- Use LinkedIn to write blog articles.
- Write articles on other platforms such as Medium, Quora, and/or your website.

- Start public speaking at conferences and/or universities associated with your company. Go ask them whether you can go to a conference and represent the company.

If you are NOT part of an association, go become part of one. Then try to speak at the associations.

Regularly share quality content related to your niche on social media – specially LinkedIn, Facebook, and Twitter. Start engaging in the right groups, forums, threads and let yourself be known.

I know some of you might find it hard to put yourself out there. My suggestion to you is this – "Don't Fear. Just be confident and put yourself out there. No one is really judging you. Frankly people don't have the time and don't care. But for those who do care like recruiters, hiring managers and others, your content will prove to become a good deal for you in the future".

The Outbound Job Search Strategy

Now we're going to talk about the outbound job search strategy. Remember that this strategy is all about you reaching out and taking control of your job search in your own hands. The strategy has the following steps:

1. **Find Target Companies** – Companies that are hiring (but may not have a position available) or companies that specifically have a position available open.
2. **Find Decision Makers** – Find people in these companies who are likely to make a hiring decision.
3. **Send them your value proposition letter.**
4. **Follow up.**

This strategy is the essence of tapping into the hidden job market. So, let's look at these in detail:

Find Target Companies

Target companies are companies that you want to get a job at. How do you find these target companies? There are three approaches that I recommend:

Find Growing Companies – These movers and shaker companies are ones that potentially may be hiring. So, for example – companies that have just been acquired or companies are about to and just gone public or companies that have merged or companies that have raised a new round of funding or companies that have a new CEO or a new department head. All these companies indicate the need to change their organization and so most likely they will be making tons of changes internally and open a bunch of positions.

How do you find these companies?

You can use Google Alerts and set up an alert to alert you each morning about what's going on in your industry and/or geographical location.

For example, you can setup alerts as follows:

- Growing Industries+Denver Colorado
- Medical Device+Corporate Expansions
- Pharmaceutical+Oncology+growth
- Consumer Goods+Acquisitions
- Growing Companies+Houston, Texas
- Private Equity Firms+Real Estate Portfolios
- IOT (internet of things) (just put the keyword in and see what happens!)

- Technology Companies+Growth+California

Then each morning as you grab coffee, you can prepare your list of target companies, ones that are growing.

Note and this is important – Companies don't need to have a position listed on their website or somewhere to be a Target Company. They simply must be a Mover or Shaker of some sort. The changes that they will hire is very high.

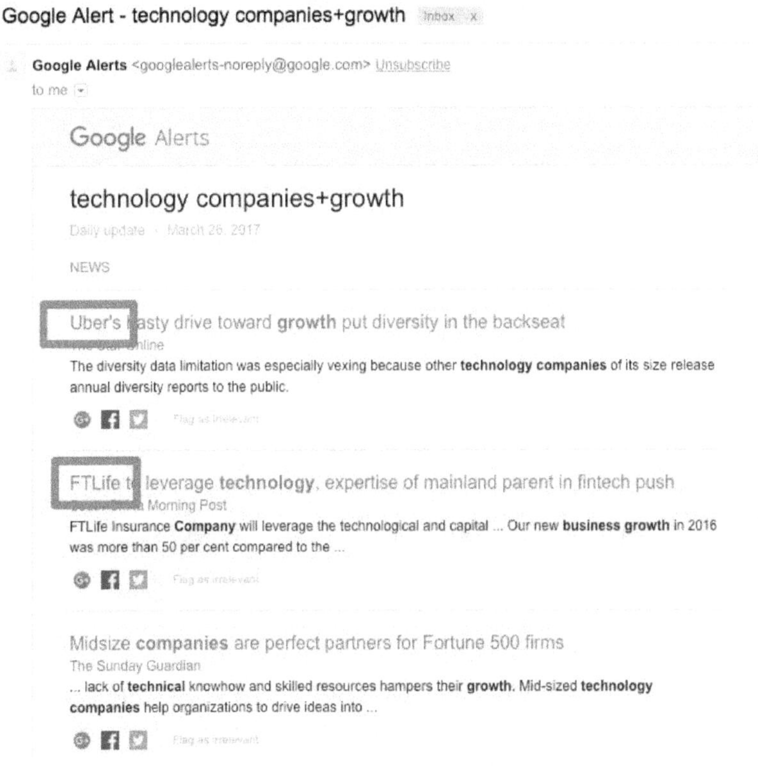

Figure 52 – Using Google Alerts to Find Companies

A second approach you can use is to setup an alert as part of a job board. In my case I prefer an aggregator job board like indeed.com. The reason is that indeed will aggregate all the jobs on the internet into one simple email and will give you a snapshot each morning. Then just like you did in the previous step, you can pick out the companies that make sense and add them to your target list. Please note that I've not asked you to apply to the position. Simply add the target company and make a note of the position they are hiring for. Do not apply to the company.

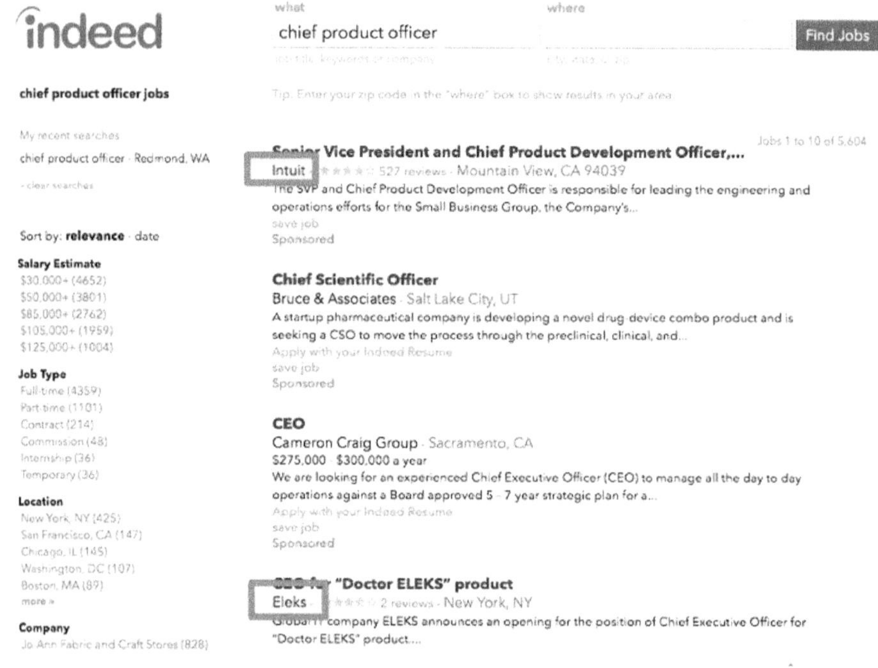

Figure 53 – Using Indeed to Look for Jobs

A final third technique is using Google Maps. Using this technique, you can look for opportunities locally in your area. Simply go to google maps and put in your search terms and you should see several different companies prop up. Again, add the ones you'd be interested to work in into your target list of companies.

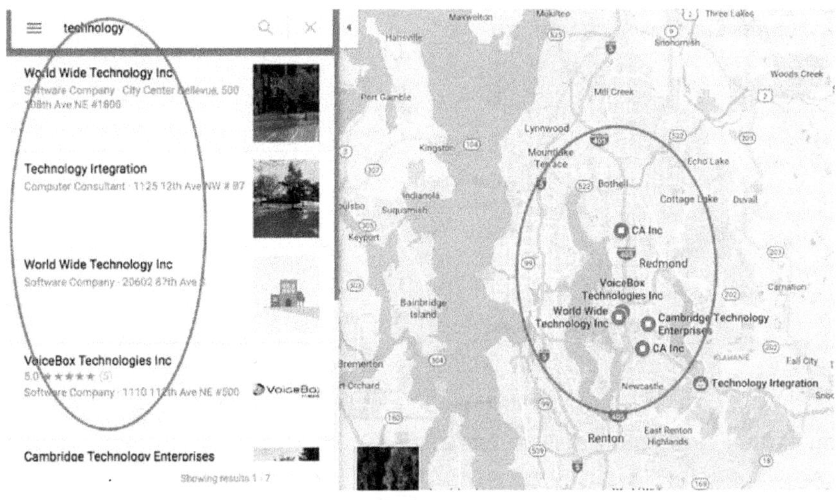

Figure 54 – Using Google Maps to Look for Jobs

Find Decision Makers

Once you've got a solid pipeline of target companies, the next step is to find decision makers in those companies. How do you find these decision makers?

Find people 2 – 3 levels above you – these are likely going to hiring you. For example: If you are an Entry to mid-level engineer.

You can find out who the:

- VP of Engineering is
- Chief Engineer is
- Engineering Design Manager is
- Company President is

Where do I find these decision makers?

It depends upon where you got the lead, but some general:

- Company website
- LinkedIn
- General Google Search
- Articles
- Paid resources
- etc.etc.etc.

Big Picture – In today's online day and age there should be NO reason for you to NOT find your decision maker ASAP.

Send Them Your Value Proposition Letter

Once you know who the decision maker is, you should send them your value proposition letter. What is the value proposition letter? A Value Proposition Letter or VPL is nothing but a very short cover letter that states to the decision maker what value you bring to the organization. It's a direct statement of why they should hire you and what you bring to their table. The VPL is very value and outcome driven, so it's important to ensure that you can clearly state your value in your value proposition letter.

How do you send the Value Proposition letter to the decision maker? Here are three approaches:

1. Direct Mail Them.
2. Email Them.
3. Send Them a LinkedIn in mail.

In my experience, the best approach is to direct mail them. As an executive, if you get a physical mail from someone trying to explain why you should be hiring them, you're sure to possibly reach back out. Of course, if you can't direct mail, then email is the next best and then a message on LinkedIn. However, Direct Mail works. Just imagine if it's your birthday and if someone sends you a physical card versus an email versus a Facebook message. You are likely to feel your best when you get a physical card in the mail. Don't underestimate the human element of the process and a physical letter can do wonders.

Here is a sample VPL that I've used in the past:

Kunal Chopra, MBA

Redmond, WA, 98053 | 425.281.3566 | kunal@coursetake.com | LinkedIn

[date]
[salute] [first] [last]
[company]
[address]
[city], [state] [zip code]

Dear [salute] [last]:

Are you looking for a COO to help you drive operational growth and profitability?

Throughout my career, I've held high-impact COO and VP roles that empowered growth-centric technology companies to achieve rapid revenue growth, generate cost savings, boost global market share, and create efficiencies.

A few specifics include:

- *Drove 15% YOY business growth.*
- *Took operating loss to 20% EBITDA improvement.*
- *Cut overall operational costs by 50%.*

If you would like to achieve similar results, I'd like the opportunity to speak to you. Although my total compensation is in north of $200,000, my primary focus is to help take a small to mid-sized B2C/B2B tech company to its next level of success.

Please call and let's explore your opportunities.

Sincerely,

Kunal Chopra, MBA

P.S. I am known for leveraging business strategy and tactical execution to achieve business success. To learn more about my achievements please see the enclosed/attached resume.

Following Up

Then you've got to follow up regularly, every week. If you get no response, then try to find another contact in the company and send them your value proposition letter.

Note that even if you see a position in the company, you should send your VPL to the decision maker. There is a high change that if your profile meets the bar, the decision maker will either reach out to you or forward your profile over to the right person.

Conclusion – The 15 Steps

So, to summarize the entire process, I've listed out 15 steps that you should follow into your career in the order described to ensure that you execute on the Inbound Outbound strategy. The reason the order is important is because for example: you don't want to reach out to a decision maker before your story and website is done. Making sense? The entire process is summarized in Figure 50.

Appendix C – Offer Evaluation and Salary Negotiation Mastery Framework

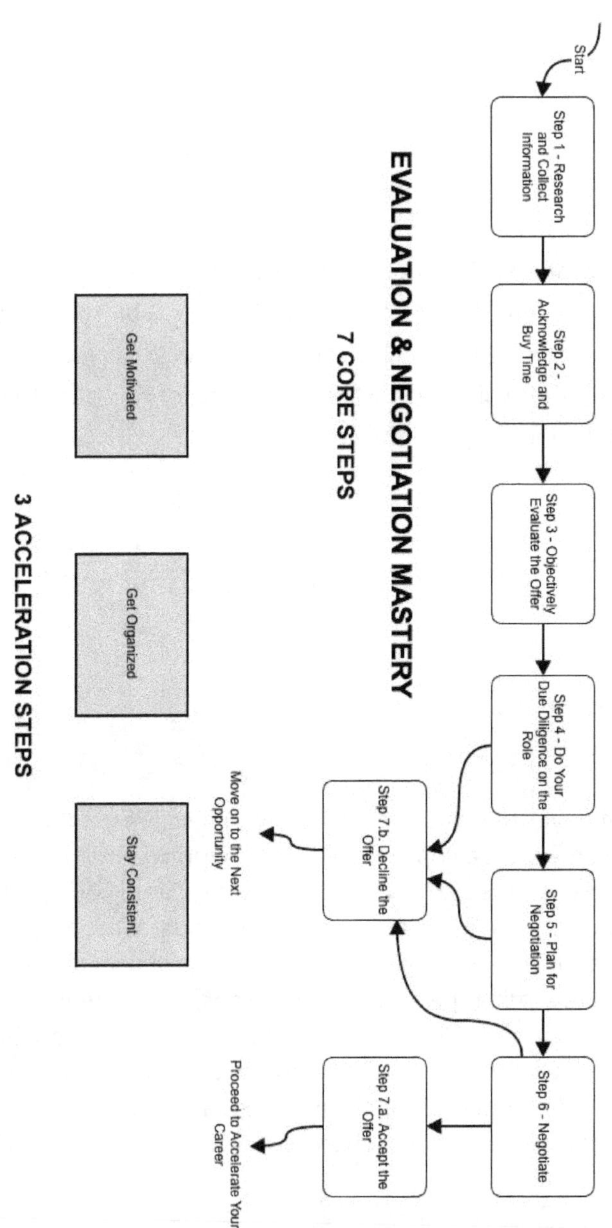

Figure 55 – The Offer Evaluation and Salary Negotiation Mastery Framework

To properly evaluate an offer put in front of you and then negotiate your package to get paid what you are worth, I recommend the following approach:

1. Start by doing through research and collecting information

You want to collect information about the company, about typical salary packages in the industry, in competitor firms etc. etc. You want to collect information about different levels and positions in the industry and within the company. This will give you the basis to calibrate your offer against the rest of the industry and the company.

2. Acknowledge, Buy Time and Consult

Acknowledge

Tell the employer that you are pleased with being made the offer, ask when you can expect a copy of the offer in writing, and find out when your response is expected. By waiting to accept until you see the offer in writing, you will have more time to make your decision. Most companies will find this to be reasonable. The offer letter will generally contain information regarding the salary, bonus plans, and benefits. You may also request information to be included such as other compensation arrangements as discussed in the interview process, details on the position's fundamental responsibilities and tasks, and any arrangements regarding relocation, compensation review dates or other specifics important to you.

If a company will not put the offer in writing, then you can put what you understand to be the offer in a letter that they need to sign/confirm. If you are unsure of the wording or legal implications of doing this, you should consult an employment attorney. If a company pushes back on placing offers in writing, or accepting your letter of understanding, you might want to consider whether this is the right firm for you. Such documents are standard business practice.

Buy Time and Consult

Once a company has made you an offer, most will want you to reply as soon as possible. However, if the offer comes at a time when you are in negotiations with other companies, you may need a little time to evaluate all the offers. Simply explain that the decision is critical to your career and that you would like some time to make your decision.

If the job change is going to require relocation, you can buy a little extra time by mentioning that you need enough time to take a final consider relocation possibilities. The employer will understand this, so you may be able to postpone your final decision for a few more days. You can use the extra days to contact the second employer and discuss any forthcoming offers. You can even explain to the second company that you have received an offer, but would like to finish your negotiations with them before making your final decision.

3.Objectively Evaluate Your Offer

Next you want to objectively evaluate the offer. As part of the career planning process, you put together your preferences, your likes and dislikes, your long-term goals, your ideal job etc. etc. Now is the time to get back to that and evaluate as to how this next move compares to your overall career plan.

A simple approach would be to use spreadsheet as shown in Figure 56 and evaluate each of your criteria against your offers. If you have a single offer, then you will want to prioritize the criteria that are the most important to you and then see how this job compares to your top criteria.

If this job scores high on the lower priority criteria and not so much on the higher items, then it may not be the best fit.

Evaluation Worksheet

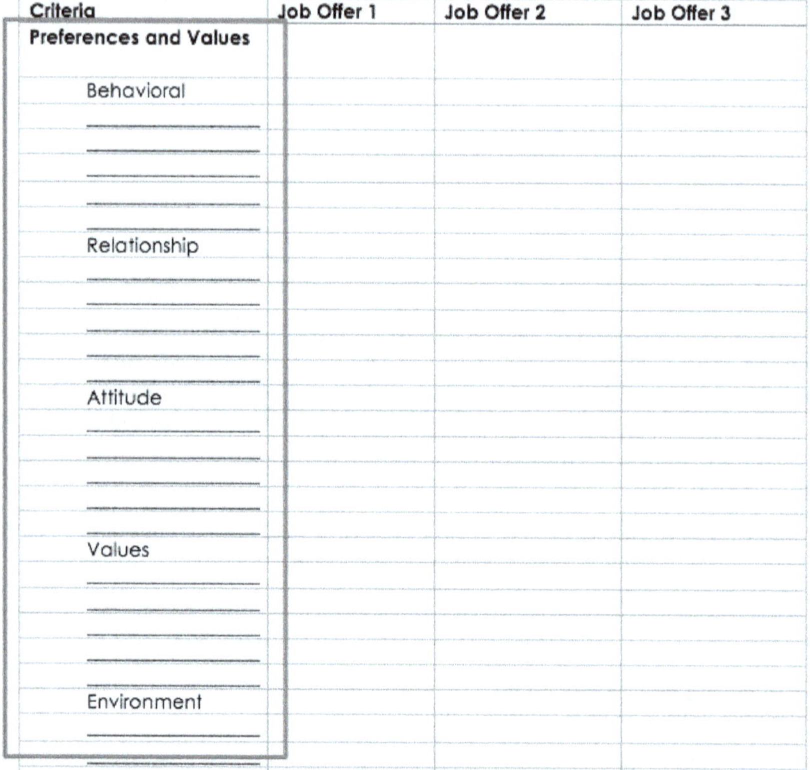

Criteria	Job Offer 1	Job Offer 2	Job Offer 3
Preferences and Values			
Behavioral			
___			
___			
___			
___			
___			
Relationship			
___			
___			
___			
___			
___			
Attitude			
___			
___			
___			
___			
___			
Values			
___			
___			
___			
___			
___			
Environment			
___			
___			

Figure 56 – Evaluation Worksheet

In addition to the evaluation worksheet, you should take some time to answer the following questions to ensure you are making a thorough and educated decision about whether to accept the offer.

1. How will the job you're about to accept help you achieve your five or ten-year goals?
2. How will your skills, personality, and talents be an asset in your new job?
3. How will the job you're about to accept help you bridge gaps in your experience?
4. Which aspects of the job will you really enjoy doing?
5. How close is this to your ideal work environment?

6. How will the new job allow you to minimize things that were de-motivators in past job(s)?
7. From what you've experienced so far, how do you feel about your coworkers and boss? Do you have any concerns, and if so, what are they?
8. Is the work and travel schedule compatible with your lifestyle?
9. How will the compensation package allow you to maintain and/or improve your current lifestyle?

At the end of this step, you should have clearer idea on whether this next role makes sense to proceed with or not.

4.Do Your Due Diligence on the Role

Managers will do a lot of selling on how good the role is and why it's the best opportunity for you. But you must do your own due diligence on whether it makes sense to join this organization.

The approach I recommend is to evaluate three risk factors using four different risk levels:

The risk factors are:

- **Organization Risk**
- **Role Risk**
- **Personal Risk**

The risk levels are:

- **1: low**
- **2: manageable**
- **3: mission-crippling**
- **4: insurmountable**

Assess overall risk and if it's

- **Relatively low**, do nothing out of the ordinary (but keep your eyes open for the inevitable changes)
- **Manageable**, manage it in the normal course of your job.
- **Mission-crippling**, resolve before accepting the job or mitigate before doing anything else.
- **Insurmountable**, walk away.

Organizational Risk

Assess risks of organization's strategy and ability to implement. Choose a number for the Organizational Risk Level: 1, 2, 3, 4

1 – Lowest

4 – Highest

(Look for the organization's sustainable competitive advantage)

1. What is the firm's **competitive** advantage?
2. Are there any risks with the current **customer** base?
3. Are there any risks with relationships with significant **collaborators** of the organization?
4. Does the organization have the **capabilities** required for long term success?
5. Do **competitors** pose significant risks to the viability of the organization?
6. Are there any outside **conditions** that will impact the viability of the organization?

Organization Risk Level: ____________________

Role Risk

Role: Assess risks of stakeholders' alignment around expectations and resources. Choose a number for the Role Risk Level: 1, 2, 3, 4

1 – Lowest

4 – Highest

(Understand who had concerns about the role and what was done to address them)

1. Did anyone have concerns about this role, and if so, what was done to mitigate them?
2. Why does this position exist? Why did the organization need to create it in the first place?
3. What are the objectives and outcomes? What are you supposed to get done? By when is it supposed to be done?
4. What will the impact be on the rest of the organization? What kind of interactions can you expect with key stakeholders?
5. What are your specific responsibilities, including decision-making authority and direct reports?

Role Risk Level: ________________________

Personal Risk

Personal: Assess risk of gaps in your strengths, motivation or fit. Choose a number for the Personal Risk Level: 1, 2, 3, 4

1 – Lowest

4 – Highest

(Understand what, specifically, about you led you're getting an offer)

1. What specifically, about me, led the organization to offer me the job?
2. Is this the company and role that can best capitalize on my strengths over time?
3. Will I look forward to coming to work three weeks, months, or years from now?

Personal Risk Level: ____________________

Overall Risk: ___________________________

Final Decision: Should I move forward with the negotiation or not?

5. Plan Your Negotiation

Now that you've decided to proceed with the negotiation, it's time to negotiate and get paid what you are worth. But before that you'll want to plan your negotiation. This is where all your research comes into play.

In this step, we'll start thinking through what are the points of the offer that you are happy with and what are the points that you don't like in order of importance. Then we'll put together an end to end plan to negotiate each item that is important to you.

Here are the three steps that you can follow:

1. Gather details about your offer.

Gather as many details about the offer as possible and ask for them in writing. (You should've done this already by now). This would include the description of the role, the reporting structure, and the compensation terms.

Rank in importance all the elements of the offer that are important to you.

Identify each of the critical elements that you will be negotiating (the ones that don't work for you).

Here are a few sample items to negotiate:

- Base Salary
- Bonus
- Stock Options
- Start Date
- Benefits (Paid Time OFF etc. etc.)
- Severance
- Relocation
- Next review date
- Next promotion
- Signing bonus

2. Plan to negotiate

- Map out your needs and concerns.
- Map out their needs and concerns.
- Identify your walkway, minimum, expected and opening points for each of the critical elements.

For each item on your list in #1, you should create something known as a Negotiation Positioning Map.

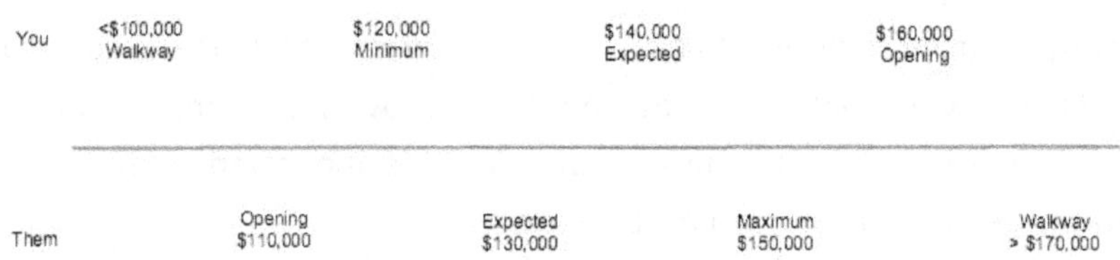

Figure 57 – Negotiation Positioning Map for Base Salary

We've used a base salary example because it's easy to illustrate.

You will want to map out on similar scales all the important dimensions of short-, mid-, and long-term compensation, benefits, termination rights, role, responsibilities, expectations, and authority.

3. Position yourself for negotiation.

List all the things as to why you believe you deserve the higher salary. Here are a few examples:

1. The current market rate for the same position.
2. What competitive companies are offering.
3. The value that you can personally bring to the organization and how you can help the company do better.
4. Your personal expenses.

etc. etc. etc.

Use this and the negotiation positioning as part of the call with your hiring manager.

6. Negotiate

Schedule time with the hiring manager to discuss your questions.

Be ready to propose alternatives to the offer terms. Think of this as a way to find a win-win situation for you and the employer. Remember that negotiation is not about winning for any side. It's about finding a compromise and is a win-win for both sides.

Look at the offer holistically – THE VALUE OF THE OFFER, not just a component of it.

Make sure to present all your considerations at the same time. Don't go back and forth multiple times on different topics.

You don't always have to negotiate. If the terms meet (or exceed) your considered expectations, and terms have been discussed throughout the interview process, you may just want to accept.

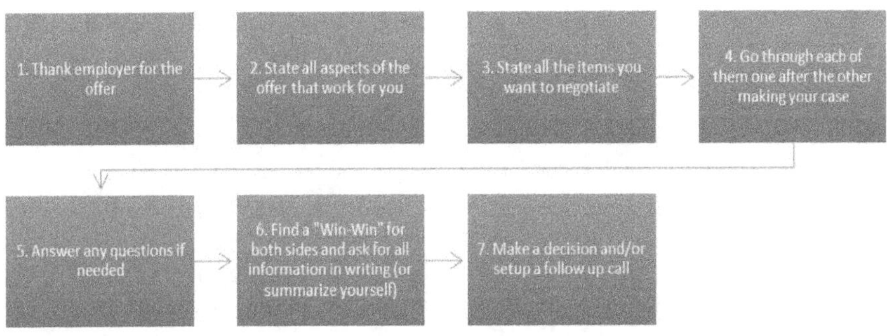

Figure 58 – General Approach to Negotiation

7. Accept or Decline the Offer

Finally, decide to accept or decline the offer based on everything you have done so far – evaluation of the offer, due diligence, and your negotiation.

Call or email your hiring manager and recruiter. Make sure you consistently communicate throughout the process.

Appendix D – Promotion Mastery

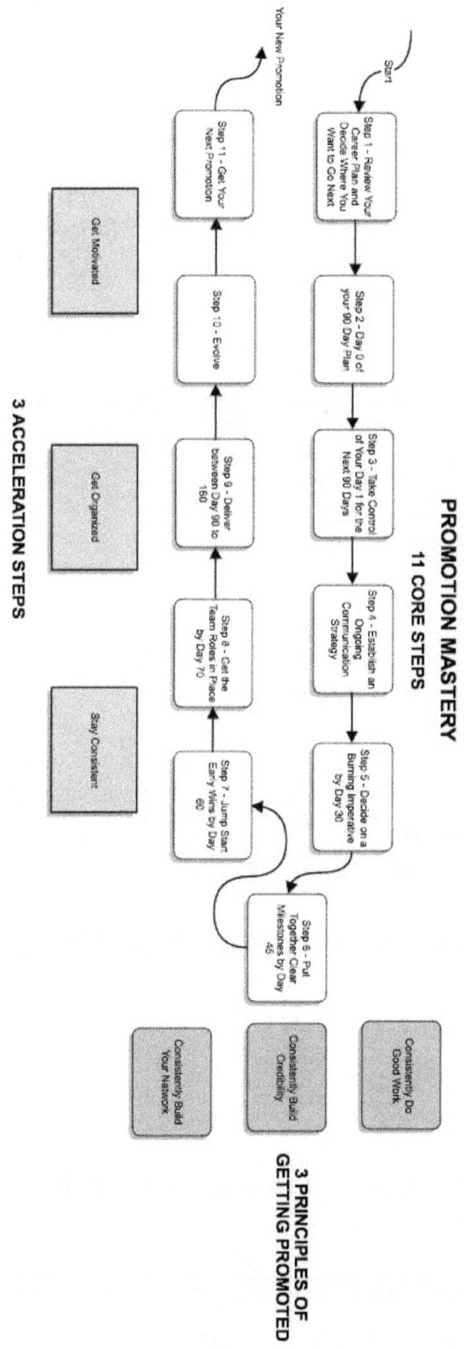

Figure 59 – The Promotion Mastery Framework

In this chapter, we'll look at what does it take to get promoted fast.

So how do you get promoted?

You get promoted when your boss and your boss's peers think that you are better than your peers.

To make them feel that you've got to follow the following three principles:

1. Do Better

Set ruthless priorities, work, and lead more strategically, and deal with frustrating obstacles and stupid people.

2. Look Better

Build your credibility with the people who can help (or blacklist) you.

3. Connect Better

Develop your network without being political. Get on the "The List" of people who get the best opportunities.

To do these three things, I've laid out 11 step promotion mastery blueprint. The steps of the blueprint are as follows:

1. Start by reviewing your career plan and decide whether it makes sense to work on a promotion or to change your job or go back to school or whatever next is in store for you to get you closer to your long-term goals.

2. Once you have that decision made and indeed you are going to stick to your current role and work towards a promotion, you'll want to put together a 90 to 180-day promotion plan. The goal of planning is to pick a project and/or projects that add tremendous value to your company and that value is of extreme importance to various stakeholders.

3. Once you've decided on a project, you'll want to sell that project proposal to the appropriate stakeholders and gain buy in.

4. Once everyone has bought into the project and you've been approved to execute, you will want to establish an ongoing communication plan on how you're going to communicate to various stakeholders on the status of the project.

5. Then you'll want to refine your plan and have a clear-cut strategy on how you're going to execute on the plan for the project. In this step, it's about adding more detail to that "value adding" project.

6. Then you'll want to put together very clear-cut milestones for your project, having crystal-clear deadlines in place.

7. Then you will want to start executing, but more importantly, you'll want to get some early wins down your throat. These early wins will establish a rhythm, will install confidence in your team and stakeholders will start trusting and believing in your ability to execute.

8. With that momentum, you'll want to expand your team and get more people involved. This means either having direct reports or building out a virtual team that you are leading. You are now showing your leadership skills to all stakeholders.

9. Deliver. Period. Do whatever it takes to deliver on the burning imperative you set out in the initial phases of this effort.

10. Evolve. This is where learning comes into play. Do debriefs with stakeholders and other members of the team. Learn from mistakes and suggest improvements for the future.

11. Finally, get promoted. Showcase to your manager and all other stakeholders all the work you did and quantify the value you brought for the company. Position yourself and ask for a promotion.

Appendix E - How to Stay Motivated Through Your Career?

In this appendix, I will detail out how to stay motivated through your career. I will specifically outline three concepts that if you grasp easily and keep in mind as you are going through your career, will help you immensely to find the dream path you seek. The three concepts are:

1. The Process is Mechanical.
2. You are the Solution to the Company's Problems.
3. You are Confident.

Let's look at these in detail next.

Get Motivated – The Process is Mechanical

The entire process is a "Game of Numbers" with "NO emotions"

- Kunal Chopra

Let's start by understanding a typical sales pipeline. Let's say that I'm a company trying to sell my products and/or services to my customers, say small to medium businesses. For me to be successful in closing deals, I will have to come up with something known as a sales pipeline. A typical sales pipeline is shown in Figure 60.

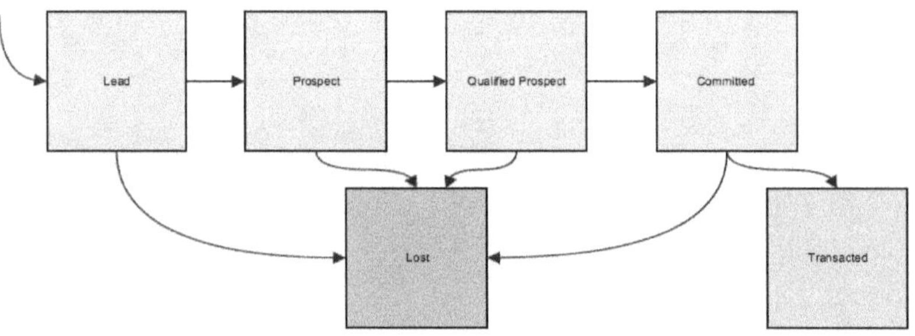

Figure 60 – The Sales Pipeline

The first step is all about finding **"Leads".** Leads are potential customers that have shown some interest in your product or service or maybe you think they could become potential customers of yours.

The next step is about converting "Leads" to **"Prospects"** – those potential customers who have shown a genuine interest in purchasing your product or service.

Prospects can further be "**Qualified**", which means you have proof that they are NOT only interested but also can pay for your product or service.

Next in the phase is "**Committed**" – these are clients who are ready to go. They have closed on the terms of the deal and are ready to sign off. You have their word.

Finally, from "Committed" you move onto "**Transacted**" where the actual deal terms are signed and the deal is closed. This is the phase in which you say, **"You've Won the Deal".**

From any given phase, you can move into the phase called "**Lost**", which means you could lose a deal – that customer doesn't want your product or service (for now).

So, what's so special about this sales pipeline?

There are three important characteristics of this process that are important:

1. **It's a mechanical process based on numbers.**
2. **It's a disciplined process.**
3. **It's a process that requires skills for you to close a deal at each phase and move it onto the next.**

1. It's a Mechanical Process Based on Numbers.

What this means is that there are **no emotions** attached to the process. At the end of the day it's all a numbers game. You find a certain number of "Leads". Some of them convert to "Prospects", some of them will be "Qualified". Some will further move to "Committed", some will "Transact" and some will be "Lost".

It's a pure game of conversion from one step to another.

2. It's a Disciplined Process

You must be **disciplined** to consistently find leads; you must be disciplined to consistently follow up with them with they don't respond.

When deals get lost, you cannot throw your arms up in the air and give up.

You must keep going.

3. It Requires Skills

At each phase in the process, you must listen to your potential customer, you must sell him or her your product or service, you must have the knack to be able to ensure that your company can deliver for them and get rid of any concerns that they might have. The better you do this, the faster you will be able to close a deal.

How do you acquire skills?

You practice, practice more and practice some more. Consistent practice is the key to being able to get skilled at something.

The Point

Salespeople consistently sell their products and services by following the process **mechanically** and **by keeping emotions out of the process**, by being **disciplined** and by **gaining skills** to be able close deals at every given point of time.

Let's compare this next to recruiting and understand the Recruiting Pipeline

Recruiting is nothing but a **sales pipeline.** You are the product and you are the salesman. The company is your customer looking to buy you. If you think about recruiting this way, we can apply the same characteristics of a sales pipeline to the recruiting pipeline.

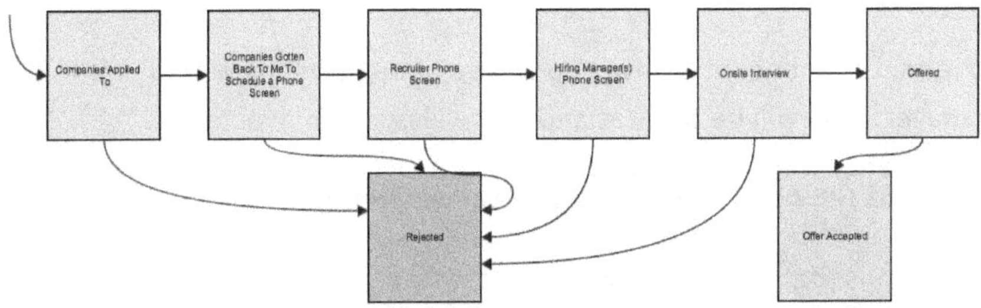

Figure 61 – The Recruiting Pipeline

For example: You start by applying to several companies. Some of these companies will get back to you to schedule a phone screen. Some of those will schedule a phone screen and you'll get to speak to a recruiter. Few of them will pass you on to the next round, which is the hiring manager screen. Some will further convert you to an onsite interview and some others will offer you a job. One of those jobs you will accept. Additionally, you could be rejected throughout the process as well.

A Slight Detour - The Concept of Conversion from One Stage to Another

Let's say that I apply to 100 jobs. Let's assume that 25% of those jobs convert into a recruiter getting back to me to schedule a phone interview. So that's a total of 25 recruiter interviews.

Let's say now that out of the 25 phone interviews 75% convert into a hiring manager phone screen. That's a total of 18 phone screens (approximately).

Now let's say that 25% of these convert into on sites. That's a total of four on sites.

Let's say 25% of those four convert to a job offer. That's one job offer.

You can clearly see that the entire process is nothing but a pipeline of conversions.

What if you start off with 200 applications?

Now you'll have:

50 recruiter phone interviews, 36 will be phone screens with the hiring manager, nine will be on sites and two will result in a job offer.

What was the point of this analysis and example?

The point is that there are two levers that you have as someone looking for a job to improve your conversion:

1. **The number of applications that you put out initially.**
2. **The conversion percentage at each stage.**

How do you impact these two levers? Well, we'll go back to the learnings from our sales pipeline and it's three important characteristics.

1. You've got to keep your emotions out of it and follow the process mechanically. You've got to think about the process in terms of numbers converting from one stage to another.

2. You've got to be disciplined to consistently find leads (companies to apply to) and to continuously follow up as and when required. This will help you increase the number of high quality applications that you put out.

3. You've got to continuously practice gaining the skills to move your product and service to the next round of the pipeline. This will help you increase your conversion percentage with each round.

My friends: Recruiting is nothing but a numbers game. You cast a wide net and you convert a certain number of customers at each phase of the pipeline and eventually you will close a deal.

This is how sales deals are done. It's no different for recruiting. Throughout the career planning process, the job search process, the interview process, the negotiation process, the acceleration process, keep in mind that you must sell. You must sell yourself to the company. You are the product and you are trying to convince the potential customer for your product that you will be able to provide value to them. If the customer is convinced that you will provide enough value, you will get the job. If not, move on to the next customer.

Get Motivated – You Are the Solution to the Company's Problems

Position Yourself as a Solution to Your Future Company's Problems

- Kunal Chopra

Organizations are full of problems. Sometimes managers know them and sometimes they do not. Whatever the case, you need to position yourself as a **solution** to those problems.

But that goes beyond the technical know-how of the job, it comes down to three specific things: **strengths, motivations, and fit.**

Through the process, right from when you start looking for your next opportunity, all the way to negotiating, reinforce these three key points to ensure that you are the **solution to the company's problems.** Emphasize your strengths, motivations, and your fit.

Next, we can translate this to interviewing. There are only three interview questions that can be asked of you during an interview.

- Can you do the job? This is testing your strengths.
- Will you love this job? This is testing your motivation.
- Can we tolerate working with you? This is testing your fit.

Any question type asked is some variation of these three types of questions.

Well, if there are only three interview questions to any job, then there are probably only three answers to any interview. As you go through your interview process, there are three things that you will need to showcase to your employer.

- **Your strengths are a match for this job.**
- **Your motivations are a match for this job.**
- **You are a good fit for this organization.**

This is outlined in Figure 62.

Let's take a few examples of questions to emphasize this point.

Tell me about yourself. **Type — Strengths**

What do you know about this company's products? **Type — Motivation**

Tell me about a time when you had to deal with conflict? **Type — Fit or Strengths (based on the Job)**

Give me an example of a time when you behaved with integrity? **Type — Fit**

Why <Company X>? **Type — Motivation**

What process do you use to prioritize a backlog? **Type — Strengths**

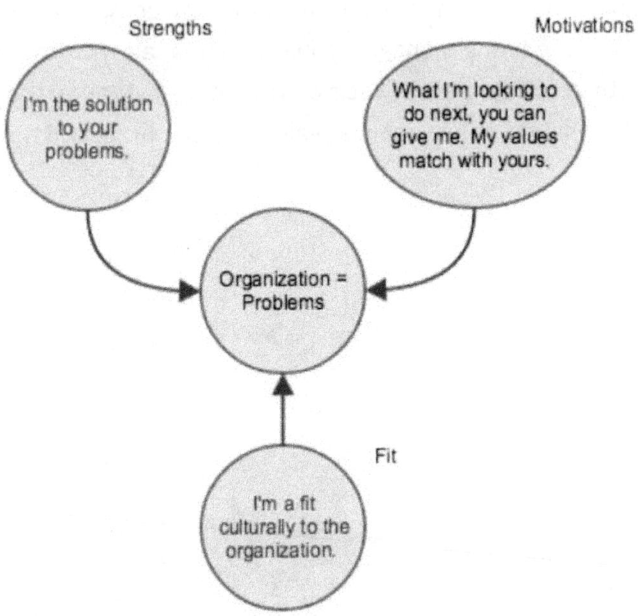

Figure 62 – Strengths, Motivations and Fit

The point here is to understand that you must consistently position yourself through the recruiting process as a solution to the organization's problems and that is done by consistently keeping in mind the concept of strengths, motivations and fit.

If you remember in the first concept, we talked about how you need to sell yourself consistently keeping emotions out of the process. This concept is all about "What do you sell?". Answer – your strengths, your motivation, and your fit.

But you can always go a level deeper and ask the question – "Who should I sell to?". In other words, "Who is the one trying to solve the problem for the organization?

Answer – The hiring manager. Not human resources, not the recruiter, not co-workers, not recruiting agencies. The person who has the closest information to the problem at hand is the hiring manager.

Why do I say this to you? Because there is one person that you must convince that you can provide everything that the company is looking for. That person is the hiring manager. Your hiring manager or future boss has the power to veto every other decision regarding giving you the job. Consistently sell him or her on what value you can bring and the job is yours.

Get Motivated – You are Confident

There is only one thing that differentiates stellar employees from the weak ones – "Confidence"

- *Kunal Chopra*

Finally, it's all about confidence. The biggest problem that candidates have when going through the career planning process:

One Word – **Nervousness**

How do you fix that?

One Word – **Confidence**

I've been interviewing candidates for many years now. The difference between the candidates that make it through and don't make it through are the ones who showcase a certain level of confidence - confidence to know what they want, confidence to say no, confidence to know the value they can provide to their organization, confidence to know their market value and negotiate well, confidence to reach out to decision makers and build relationships with them, however senior they may be, confidence to move past rejections that they might get through the process, etc. etc. The confident candidate always wins, time and time again.

So, the question that you must ask yourself is simple – "How confident are you?" when it comes to your career planning process. Are you one who can stand straight and hold your head up high in the face of challenges, or are you the kind of person who will throw up his or her hands up in the air when things don't go your way? Whatever the case may be, you need confidence to truly do concepts one and two in this chapter; i.e. to sell yourself and sell your strengths, motivations, and fit to the hiring manager.

So how do you work on your confidence? Let's look at six things that you can do right now that will help you with your confidence. I'd like you to apply these consistently every day to your career, however, at minimum, please apply them to when you are executing on any one given step of the 5x3 Dream Career Blueprint.

1. Remove your Fear of Rejection

The first thing you need to do is remove your fear of rejection. No, things are not going to go your way. Yes, you are going to get rejected from your dream company. Yes, you are going to fail ate interviews. Good. Now that you know that, just move on. Remove any fear that comes along with rejection, keep your eye on the prize and keep executing day in and day out.

You will only get your dream career fulfilled if you do not stop. If you stop, for sure you won't get it. So, do not stop.

Remember the concept of "Strengths, Motivations and Fit". Remember the concept of "The Game of Numbers". If you do not get the job you really wanted, it has nothing to do with you. It has nothing to do with you. If just means that there was a misalignment in what the company wanted and what you can provide to them. Learn from that and move onto the next thing.

2. Work Out

Believe it or not, **getting exercise during the recruiting process** is one of the best tips you'll ever receive. Not only does exercise **help relieve tension, nervousness, and help reduce stress,** but it also has scientifically proven benefits that can help you do well on any interview. Not to mention, it will help you retain information better, give you more energy, and help you network and answer questions better.

You don't have to go crazy. Just workout every day.

3. Be Patient

I'm sure you've heard the "I'll get you a job in two weeks" gurus. Yes, I wish it were that easy. To truly get your dream job you've got to be patient. The process takes time – at minimum 12 weeks, but at times could be longer. Sometimes six months to a year. Be patient and focused.

If you follow everything I've listed out here, you should have a complete plan for your career, so there should be no reason that you stay without doing something consistently. For example – networking, going to events, building up your brand, thought leadership, etc.

4. Look Good

From an interviewer's perspective looking good during an interview is going to make a huge difference in selecting a candidate. As much as you read every day in the media that companies shouldn't be judgmental when it comes to selecting candidates based on appearance, there is an inherent human bias that you just cannot eliminate.

But the benefits of looking good go beyond just the interview process. They help with your confidence. Through the process of recruiting, interviewing, negotiating etc. etc. start looking good – dress up well, take care of your hair/skin, your health, sleep well, eat well and watch how things will fall in your plate.

5. Eat Healthy

Try to avoid over eating during this time and get in some healthy food. Just like exercise has the benefits of helping you with your confidence, so does healthy food.

Healthy food will make you feel good, make you feel light, and give you the energy boost you are looking for during your interviews.

It will also help you focus and concentrate better as you retain more information.

6. Meditate (or Get Some Quite Time)

This again might be a tough one for some, but if you can get five minutes of meditation each day you will be golden.

Meditation will calm you down and reduce your stress. Meditation will help you focus on your breathing.

If you can't meditate, at least get some deep breathing, or get some quiet/piece time away from the distractions and chaos of the world.

So, there you go my friends. Use these six tips to help you increase your confidence and go take your career to its next milestone of success.

But as I've mentioned multiple times before, it's not just enough to read the things you need to do. You also need to do them. So, this is your chance to now write down things that you are going to do to help with your confidence.

Homework

Using the "Getting your Confidence Right" worksheet, write down the things you are going to do to work on your confidence.

Going forward do these things every day (or every week), till you get your new career going to its next level.

"Getting your Confidence Right" Worksheet

Check off the things that you will do to get your mind right over the next eight to 12 weeks, till you get your new job offer. Additionally, write down any items that you think would help you during your transition. Make sure to get these scheduled on a day to day basis on your calendar.

- **Workout**
- **Meditate**
- **Go for a walk**
- **Stop drinking**
- **Stop smoking**
- **Eat healthy**
- **Watch a movie twice a week**
- **Play with the kids**
- **Play a sport**
- ___________
- ___________
- ___________
- ___________
- ___________
- ___________

Appendix F – How to Stay Organized Through Your Career?

The best employees are those who are motivated, are organized, and who show up consistently

- *Kunal Chopra*

In appendix E, we focused on making sure that you stay motivated throughout your career. At the highest level, there were three concepts that we discussed:

1. The Process is Mechanical.
2. You are the Solution to the Company's Problems.
3. You are Confident.

But all this is fine in theory. How do you make this practical?

The easiest way to do so is by getting organized and you can get organized by scheduling dedicated time on your calendar.

The difference between overachievers and others, in my opinion is that the overachievers take massive action regularly. But in this busy world, with work, kids, social media etc. etc. how do you take massive action regularly? You do it by scheduling every activity on your calendar. That's exactly what this phase is about. It's about taking scheduling time on your calendar to complete your career activities regularly.

You can use any calendar software that you'd like, but I recommend Google Calendar – it's free to use and you can start scheduling your sessions immediately, get reminders, and hold yourself accountable.

You can go to calendar.google.com and get started.

Plan your activities for **1-2 hours a day** – preferably early in the morning when your mind is fresh and ready to go.

If you have studying specific activities, try to do it a **quiet place**, away from kids, friends, or any other distractions.

I know this is difficult given that you have classes, or work or a busy day – but just remember that **discipline is what is required now.**

Types of Calendars

There are **two types of calendars** that I recommend that you put together.

1. **Ongoing Calendar** – During your entire career process, I'd want you to put together a calendar to spend some time every day where you are doing activities that are common throughout the process and apply to any job and/or company that you might be in conversations with.

2. **Company/Job Specific Calendar** – Then once you have conversations scheduled with a company, I want you to back track from your meeting date and put a last-minute calendar together to help you prepare and practice for **THAT specific meeting**. Think of this as a revision session from what you learned in 1.

Why this approach of studying upfront?

Remember what we said earlier about conversion in the recruiting pipeline and how success in the entire job search process can be improved by improving your conversion rate.

Just imagine that you are applying for jobs and one day you get an email from a recruiter/hiring manager asking to schedule an interview tomorrow.

The last thing you want is to be caught off-guard and miss this interview opportunity. You want to be prepared and answer every question in detail with confidence.

Preparing early, irrespective of whether you have an interview scheduled or not, will help you move opportunities to the next stage faster in your recruiting pipeline.

Also, note that you cannot create your entire calendar upfront. It's an ongoing process as you schedule interviews and is based on your individual schedule.

You must log into your calendar daily and make updates.

Homework

It's time now to get your calendar in place. Do the following:

Using a calendar of your choice, or google calendar, please setup your ongoing calendar. Then as your situation changes, as you start getting meetings with companies, start building up your company/job specific calendar.

You can use instructions in worksheet "Get Organized".

Get Organized Worksheet

1. Google calendar is a freely available tool that you can use to create your recruiting calendar.

2. Please go to calendar.google.com and sign in (if you have a google account) or create a new one (it's free).

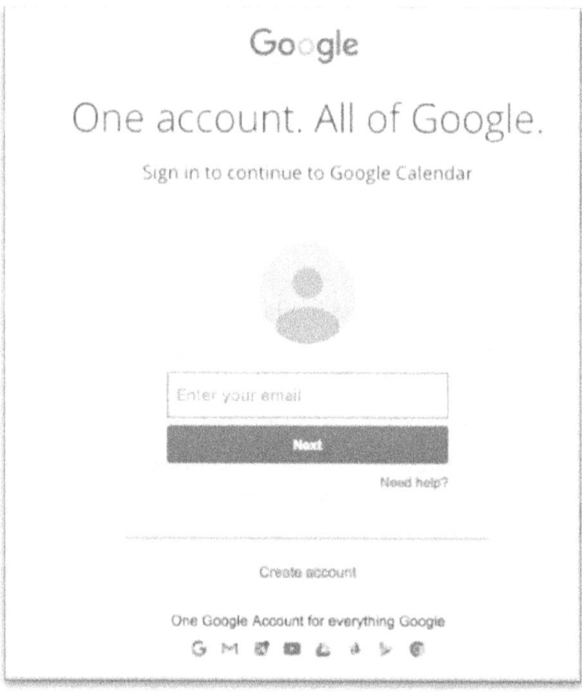

Figure 63 – Google Calendar Sign In

3. Once you log in, you should be able to create new calendar event using the "Create" button.

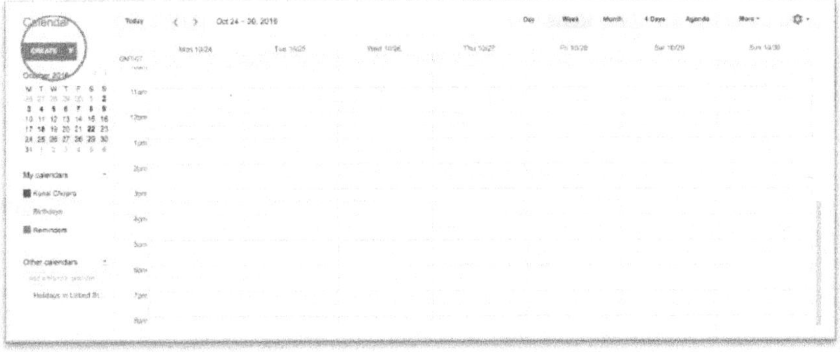

Figure 64 – Create a New Event in Google Calendar

4. **For weeks one and two (at minimum) – Set up your Ongoing Recruiting Calendar.**

   a. At minimum, set up the following:

      a. Time to work out/walk (or anything else to get your mind right).
      b. Time to create/review your career plan.
      c. Time to create/update your story.
      d. Time to update your recruiting pipeline.
      e. Time to update status of upcoming meetings.
      f. Time to research the industry.
      g. Time to create/update your target list of companies.
      h. Time to study job descriptions.
      i. Time to practice generic interview questions and answers.
      j. Time to create/update your resume/cover letter.
      k. Time to network – in person, online etc.
      l. Time to apply to companies.
      m. Time to follow up – email, messages etc.

5. **For other weeks, set up your Company/Job Recruiting Calendar**. Going forward, every day log in to adjust your calendar based on any interviews that have been scheduled and update your calendar appropriately.

a. Time to study the company you are interviewing for.
b. Time to study the job description.
c. Time to study questions to ask.
d. Time to revise everything before the interview e.g. questions/answers, your story.

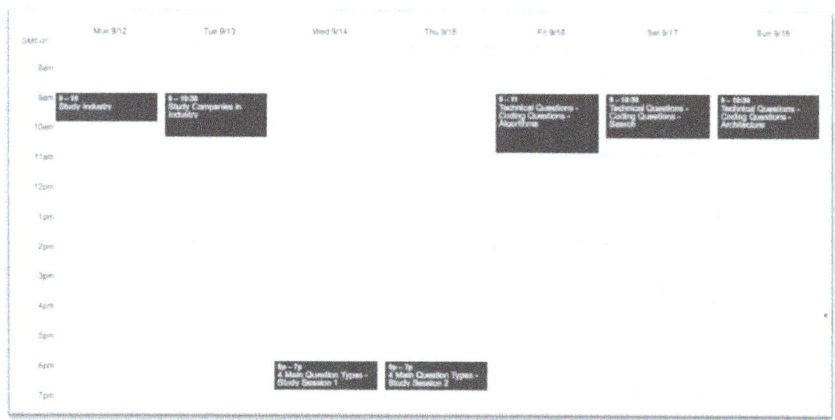

Figure 65 – Ongoing Recruiting Calendar in Google Calendar

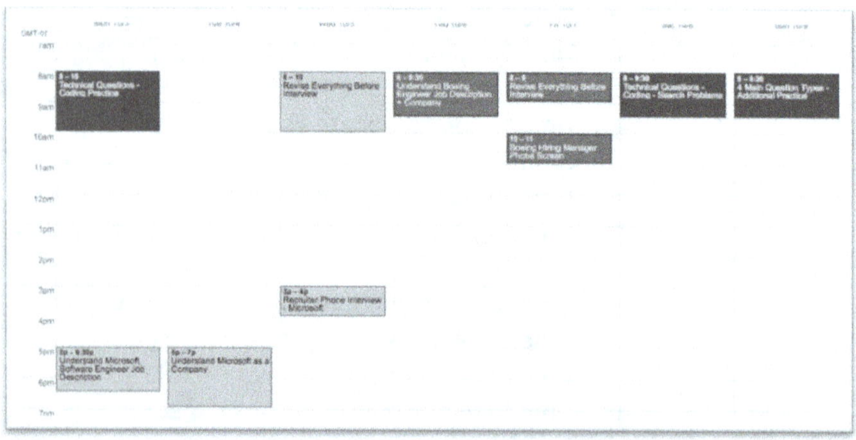

Figure 66 – Company/Job Specific Recruiting Calendar in Google Calendar

6. Consistently log in everyday and update your calendar based on your situation.

Appendix G – How to Stay Consistent Through Your Career?

In this appendix, I'll give you a framework for you to think about staying consistent your entire career.

In appendix E, we discussed how to stay motivated through your career. In appendix F, we discussed how to stay organized.

But let's be honest. Things come up and we can easily get off track in our lives. When things don't go our way, we might just give up and move on with our regular life, forgetting about those goals that we so wanted to achieve as part of our career plan.

So, how do you stay motivated in your career? How do you ensure that you can keep yourself going every day even when you don't feel like executing? In Figure 67, I've given you a framework for the same.

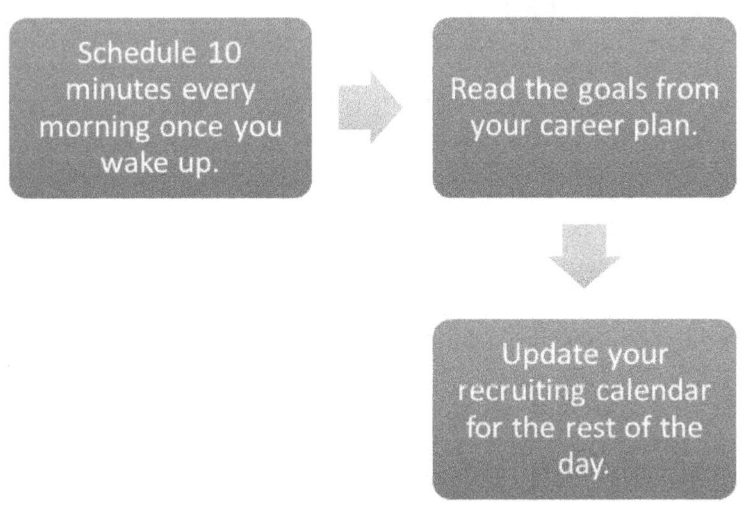

Figure 67 – How to Stay Consistent Through Your Career?

There are three steps as part of this process:

1. First things first, I'd love for you to schedule 10 minutes every day on your calendar every morning. This is something you will have to do first thing when you wake up in the morning. You've got to do this before you say hi to the kids or check your email or even brush your teeth. Simply, get your day started with these first 10 minutes.

2. Then, I'd like you to look at your goals that you've defined as part of your career plan. Read them to yourself and internalize them every morning. Focus on them as if you've already achieved them.

3. Then go execute, open your recruiting calendar, and rearrange your calendar; i.e. update it to reflect any activities that have been happening. For example: if you need to email a hiring manager, schedule it. If your meeting got moved, update your calendar etc.

I know that this might feel like there is a lot to do, but trust me – it's only with consistent focus and dedication that you will achieve your dreams. This little technique is a great way for you to get focused on your life and your career. It will ensure that you are consistently on track, every day of your life.

So, give it a try and start seeing progress towards your goals.

References

1. Rise: 3 Practical Steps for Advancing Your Career, Standing Out as a Leader, and Liking Your Life, Keith Ferrazzi

2. Corporate Confidential: 50 Secrets Your Company Doesn't Want You to Know---and What to Do About Them, Cynthia Shapiro

3. Secrets to Winning at Office Politics: How to Achieve Your Goals and Increase Your Influence at Work, Marie G. Mcintyre

4. The New Leader's 100-Day Action Plan: How to Take Charge, Build or Merge Your Team, and Get Immediate Results, George B. Bradt, Jayme A. Check, John A. Lawler

5. Execution Premium, Robert S. Kaplan and David P. Norton

www.ingramcontent.com/pod-product-compliance
Lightning Source LLC
Chambersburg PA
CBHW050158230526
45470CB00001B/148

* 9 7 8 1 9 7 8 4 9 3 7 9 7 *